THE REFERENCE SHELF VOLUME 44 NUMBER 4

REPRESENTATIVE AMERICAN SPEECHES: 1971-1972

EDITED BY WALDO W. BRADEN

Professor of Speech
Louisiana State University

THE H. W. WILSON COMPANY

NEW YORK **1972**

42221

THE REFERENCE SHELF

The books in this series contain reprints of articles, excerpts from books, and addresses on current issues and social trends in the United States and other countries. There are six separately bound numbers in each volume, all of which are generally published in the same calendar year. One number is a collection of recent speeches; each of the others is devoted to a single subject and gives background information and discussion from various points of view, concluding with a comprehensive bibliography. Books in the series may be purchased individually or on subscription.

REPRESENTATIVE AMERICAN SPEECHES: 1971-1972

Copyright © 1972

By The H. W. Wilson Company

International Standard Book Number 0-8242-0467-0

Library of Congress Catalog Card Number (38-27962)

PREFACE

"The nation's regard for its leaders, particularly political leaders, has sunk to an alarmingly low level. . . . Today's leaders seem to have less stature than their predecessors," says feature writer A. James Reichley of *Fortune* magazine (September 1971). This dearth of promising leaders is reflected in public address today, particularly in political speaking, which continues at a low ebb.

The primaries absorbed the rhetorical energies of the many presidential hopefuls. President Nixon encountered little threat from Representative Paul N. McCloskey, Jr., a liberal from California, or from Representative John M. Ashbrook, a conservative from Ohio. It took only the first primary in New Hampshire for McCloskey to spend $130,000 and exhaust his funds.

The onrush of Democratic hopefuls indicated how fragmented that party was. Because of the number of primaries, the contenders dissipated their energies and resources in attempts to gain sufficient attention to have a chance for the nomination. The fifteen actively wooing the voters were Birch Bayh, Shirley Chisholm, Fred R. Harris, Vance Hartke, Harold Hughes, Hubert H. Humphrey, Henry Jackson, John V. Lindsay, Eugene J. McCarthy, George McGovern, Wilbur D. Mills, Patsy T. Mink, Edmund S. Muskie, George Wallace, and Sam Yorty. Edward Kennedy, much discussed as a possibility, maintained that he was not interested in the nomination.

James Reston of the New York *Times* (November 17, 1971) thought that the campaign during the fall was "flat and dull" because the candidates were "working underground on the substructure of the campaign" and were "not polishing sentences, but organizing teams and gathering funds."

3

The size of the campaign chest determined how long an aspirant could continue in the race. Hughes, Harris, and Bayh dropped out early. At least in early primaries, many politicians turned to thirty-second, one-minute, and five-minute spot TV commercials to reach the voters. Image-building became important. In Florida eleven candidates spent over one million dollars among them. Well behind in the final vote, John V. Lindsay spent over $300,000, of which $180,000 went for broadcasts. Much of the stumping was dependent upon what *Newsweek* (April 17, 1972) called "word of mouth, doorbell pushing and canvassing." Rapidly decreasing financial support caused several of the contestants to change their methods and to ponder whether TV commercials were not highly overrated. The amount of money spent on TV exposure seemed to have little relation to the number of votes polled.

Eugene McCarthy tested the water briefly in Illinois. After Wisconsin, the Democratic struggle became a three-way contest among Humphrey, Muskie, and McGovern. Upon receiving serious setbacks in Pennsylvania and Massachusetts, Muskie, who had started out the front runner but who had slipped to a poor third in late April, decided "to withdraw from active participation in the remaining primaries." He had not been any more successful than McGovern and Wallace, who conducted in many states what were called "peekaboo" campaigns, meaning that the campaigner made a few speeches at stragetic spots and then hurried on to the next state.

Late primaries (those in Indiana and Ohio, for example) pointed to Humphrey and McGovern as serious contenders for the Democratic nomination, but conservative George Wallace, perhaps more an annoyance than a threat, had a sizable number of delegates under tight control. The tragic shooting of Wallace in Maryland on May 15 further complicated the contest for delegates. During the weeks prior to the Democratic convention, McGovern, far outdistancing his competitors, hoped for a first-ballot nomination.

Meanwhile, back in Washington, congressional activity droned on at a petty pace. The House was stirred to vigorous debate over the proposed prayer amendment, with Mrs. Ben Ruhlin of Ohio leading a powerful lobby in support of the bill. On November 8, 1971, representatives debated earnestly the wisdom of adding a prayer amendment to the Constitution. The affirmative was upheld by Chalmers P. Wylie (Republican, Ohio), Del Clawson (Republican, California), and Richard H. Ichord (Democrat, Missouri). The opposition was led by Emanuel Celler (Democrat, New York), Fred Schwengel (Republican, Iowa), Father Robert F. Drinan (Democrat, Massachusetts), Chet Holifield (Democrat, California), and Bella Abzug (Democrat, New York). This debate is discussed further in the section entitled "Contemporary Moods: Sacred and Profane."

The Senate as a whole heard little notable speaking, but the sessions of some committees were lively and exciting. Absenteeism handicapped the conduct of Senate business. In December, Senator Margaret Chase Smith (Republican, Maine), known as "the conscience of the Senate," expressed indignation at the poor attendance and asserted the Senate had become "a mere springboard to those who would use it —even abuse it—for their selfish interests, whether such interests be commercializing their position and title with the acquisition of high-price lecture fees or running for President. . . . Too many senators have chronic absences because they are on lecture tours piling up annual lecture incomes that even exceed their Senate salaries." She called for a constitutional amendment requiring the expulsion of any member who missed 40 percent of the votes of a session. Giving credence to what Mrs. Smith said, Majority Leader Mike Mansfield (Democrat, Montana) on February 9 expressed his exasperation with his colleagues: "What this Senate is degenerating into . . . is a three-day-a-week body. We are all becoming members of the Tuesday and Thursday club, inclusive" (*Congressional Record,* February 9, 1972, pages S 1528-9).

The speeches of President Richard M. Nixon have been in a much lower key since the close of the 1970 campaign. In the period covered by this volume (1971-1972), he used his important speeches mainly to enunciate significant developments or changes in policy. On July 6, 1971, before the midwestern newspaper executives in Kansas City, Missouri, he announced that he would "take the first step toward ending the isolation of Mainland China." On July 15, he announced on television his visit to the People's Republic. On August 15, via television, he told the nation of the new program of temporary wage and price control. Before a joint session of Congress on September 9, he presented the outline of his proposed wage-price freeze. One month later, on October 7, he gave a television speech on Phase II of his economy program. In December he welcomed Dan Rather of CBS to the White House for an interview designed to give the viewers a close look at his personal routines and views. Perhaps his most notable speech of the year was his State of the Union Message of January 20, a speech presented in this volume.

A memorable little speech, because of the occasion, not the content, was the toast that Nixon made while in China at the dinner in Shanghai on February 27. It was beamed across space by satellite. George Wallace's showing in the Florida primary stirred the President to deliver a fifteen-minute television speech denouncing school busing on March 16. On April 14, the President, eager to improve relations with our northern neighbor, delivered a carefully prepared address to a joint meeting of the Canadian Parliament in Ottawa. The increase in the tempo of the war and the resumption of large-scale bombing in Vietnam necessitated speeches on the nights of April 26 and May 8—probably the President's most dramatic efforts of the year.

Reporters continued to puzzle over the question of the real character of President Nixon, and in return the Administration continued to accuse the mass media of biased reporting and maliciousness. *Newsweek* (January 3, 1972) thought that the President "appeared more confident, more at ease," but "as ever an extremely private person." It noted that "there was the same old tendency to seize a momentary—and cheap—political advantage." Another detractor, John Osborne of the *New Republic* (January 15, 1972), said, "Mr. Nixon comes across . . . as a President who, in defensive response to the negative view, has constructed a false image of himself." Discussing the Rather interview, Osborne conceded that the President "came off quite well," but, Osborne continued, "there were little touches, petty flaws and contradictions that in their way were as revealing as the passages— and there were many—in which the President appeared to be credible and likable."

On the whole the rhetoric of the President often seemed forced, lacked inspiration, and probably did little to enhance his image. Nevertheless, the President had increased his popularity with the voters, mainly because of his visits to China and Russia and his policy of withdrawing troops from Indochina.

Continuing to fill many speaking engagements, Vice President Agnew exercised more restraint in his utterances than he did during 1969 and 1970. It had been rumored that Republican policy makers counseled him to avoid inflammatory outbursts. Popular with conservatives and right-wing Republicans, Agnew has criss-crossed the country on speaking assignments, serving as the "Administration program salesman, . . . diplomat, Republican fund-raiser and what one White House man calls 'the bayonet of the GOP' " (James P. Cannon, *Wall Street Journal,* May 5, 1972). During his tenure as Secretary of the Treasury, John B. Connally, a conservative Democrat, was called upon to speak in behalf of the Administration's economic policies. (See speech delivered to American Society of Newspaper Editors, April 19, 1972, quoted in *U.S. News & World Report,* May 1, 1972.)

The most dynamic speaking of the year took place at public meetings of disadvantaged, economically deprived, ethnic, and women's groups. The consumer and citizen activists (Nader and Common Cause), women, youth, blacks, Chicanos, Indians, and hyphenated groups such as Japanese-Americans argued for a voice in the nation's political and social processes. Speeches from these groups were much more abundant than in previous years: Many of these groups are now well organized and have found vigorous and fluent leadership.

During the year women such as Shirley Chisholm, Bella Abzug, Patsy Mink, Gloria Steinem, Caroline Bird, Eleanor Holmes Norton, Aileen C. Hernandez, Wilma Scott Heide, and Lucy W. Benson spoke effectively and forcefully. Representatives Chisholm and Abzug (Democrats, New York) promoted the National Women's Political Caucus. (See Bella Abzug's speech in this volume.) Shirley Chisholm reported that she visited forty-three states and sixty-five campuses before she launched her campaign for the Democratic nomination.

Senator Smith's chiding of her colleagues over their "high-price lecture fees" points to an important aspect of speaking activity today. Colleges and universities continue to provide an attractive forum for reformers and those who wish to support themselves by speaking. (See comment in REPRESENTATIVE AMERICAN SPEECHES: 1970-1971, pages 5-6.) The enfranchisement of eighteen-year-olds has made college audiences more important, politically. Robert P. Walker, president of the American Program Bureau, one of the largest lecture agencies, reports "that radical speakers, who were attractive during the past decade are on the wane and that college students are increasingly interested in listening to speakers who know politics from the inside out" (Edwin Roberts, Jr., *National Observer*, January 8, 1972; see also New York *Times*, December 16, 1971). Lecture fees range from $500 to $4,000 for a forty-five-minute talk, and some lecturers are making as much as $150,000 to $200,000 a year. The American Program Bureau in 1970 had bookings of $4 million. Walker asserts that he could guarantee Spiro Agnew a half million a year for lecturing, if the Vice President were willing to accept bookings. Lecture committees looking for speakers find such figures as Dick Gregory, Shirley Chisholm, Ralph Abernathy, Julian Bond, William F. Buckley, Pierre Salinger, Joyce Brothers, John Glenn, Jr., Birch Bayh, Mark Hatfield, Jack Anderson, David Brinkley, James Reston, Tom Wicker, and John Barth among those available.

Without the help and advice of many persons, I could not have completed this volume. The speakers have been most generous in supplying speech texts, background information, and biographical data. I am much indebted to Ruth Arrington and Gil Fites of Oklahoma Northeastern State College; Clark S. Carlile and Charles E. Bilyea of Idaho State University; Robert R. Boren of Boise State College; A. Craig Baird of the University of Iowa; Robert Jeffrey of the University of Texas; Elizabeth Carr of the University of Hawaii; David Cornell of Davidson College; and Roberta Madden of the Louisiana State University Press. As always, I have received valuable assistance from my departmental colleagues, especially Clinton Bradford, Stephen Cooper, Francine Merritt, Harold Mixon, and Owen Peterson. Barbara Walsh has been most resourceful in finding stray facts and in helping with preparation of the manuscript. I have indeed been fortunate to have two excellent secretaries, Carolyn Russell and Linda Michelli.

WALDO W. BRADEN

Baton Rouge, Louisiana
July 1972

CONTENTS

DIRECTIONS AND PURPOSES

STATE OF THE UNION MESSAGE, 1972 [1]

Richard M. Nixon [2]

The State of the Union Message gives the President an opportunity to present his program to the Congress and the nation. Following the custom of his recent predecessors, President Nixon chose to deliver personally his four-thousand-word message to the joint session of the Senate and the House at noon, January 20, 1972, while television cameras transmitted it to the public. In addition, Nixon handed the Vice President and the House Speaker a fifteen-thousand-word supplement, giving additional details of the ninety Administration proposals still awaiting congressional action. A State of the Union Message is of course more the pronouncement of an Administration than of a single individual; consequently it is the product of careful analysis and much discussion by top officials, advisers, and a staff of ghostwriters. There is little reason to believe that this address was prepared any differently from others of recent years.

Aware of the necessity of improving his image and of providing a base for the coming campaign, President Nixon, relaxed and confident, was more conciliatory and generous than he had been on previous occasions. In contrast to the 1971 State of the Union address, in which he made an emotional plea for "a new American Revolution" and attempted to overpower the opposition by the force of rhetoric, in 1972 President Nixon seemed "more willing to share responsibility for the past and willing to share credit for the future" (Jude Wanniski, *National Observer,* January 29, 1972). The *Christian Science Monitor* (January 24, 1972) declared that the speech was "low key"; the *Wall Street Journal* (January 21, 1972) thought that it was "more matter of fact. . . . a reasonably honest account of the Union's state." James Reston of the New York *Times,* not always generous in his comments about the President, noted: "He avoided the hard questions, but his speech had scope and dignity, and in its closing passages, a certain nobility of phrase and manner." Reston declared that it was "a graceful speech with less partisan rancor in it than in most such talks at the beginning of an election year."

[1] Delivered to a joint session of Congress, Washington, D.C., January 20, 1972.

[2] For biographical note, see Appendix.

A. James Reichley, writing in *Fortune* (September 1971), characterized President Nixon as follows: "At best . . . he comes across as a conscientious and intelligent family lawyer, who can be trusted to pursue a reasonable course. When he seeks to play a more dramatic role, he is likely to appear erratic or insincere." Much of the President's style of public address is pedestrian; when he tries flights of eloquence, he has difficulty making his words ring with purpose and sincerity. His speech writers have failed to capture his natural style or to cast his speeches into an appealing form. Too often the President's smile and manner appear forced, his gestures and movements seem stereotyped.

The question may be asked why the State of the Union Message was chosen for this compilation over some of the President's more dramatic efforts—for example, his address to the nation on May 8 in which he announced a blockade of North Vietnam. The latter speech was indeed dramatic and may have far-reaching repercussions. But the State of the Union Message is broader in scope and gives an overview of the directions and purposes of the Nixon Administration. In a word, the speech is a credo of the Republicans and the President. Some observers have concluded that by this speech the President has taken away the middle ground from the Democrats. Many believe that the President hopes to make this message the guide for his campaign for reelection, depending, of course, upon the turn of events in Southeast Asia.

Mr. Speaker, Mr. President, my colleagues in the Congress, our distinguished guests and my fellow Americans:

Twenty-five years ago I sat here as a freshman congressman—along with Speaker Albert—and listened for the first time to the President address us on the State of the Union.

I shall never forget that moment. The Senate, the Diplomatic Corps, the Supreme Court, the Cabinet entered the chamber, and then the President of the United States. As all of you are aware, I had some differences with President Truman, as he did with me. But I remember that on the day he addressed that joint session of the newly elected Republican Congress, he spoke not as a partisan but as President of all the people—calling upon the Congress to put aside partisan considerations in the national interest.

The Greek-Turkish aid program, the Marshall Plan, the great foreign policy initiatives which have been responsible for avoiding a world war for the past twenty-five years were approved by that Eightieth Congress, by a bipartisan majority of which I was proud to be a part.

Nineteen seventy-two is before us. It holds precious time in which to accomplish good for this nation. We must not waste it. I know the political pressures in this session of the Congress will be great. There are more candidates for the presidency in this chamber today than there probably have been at any one time in the whole history of the Republic. There is an honest division of opinion, not only between the parties but within the parties, on some issues of foreign policy and domestic policy as well.

However, there are great national problems that are so vital they transcend partisanship. Let us have our debates. Let us have our honest differences. But let us join in keeping the national interest first. Let us join in making sure that legislation the nation needs does not become hostage to the political interest of any party or any person.

There is ample precedent, in this election year, for me to present you with a huge list of new proposals, knowing full well that there could be no possibility that they could be enacted even if you worked night and day.

I shall not do that.

I have presented to the leaders of the Congress today a message of 15,000 words discussing in some detail where the nation stands and setting forth specific legislative items on which I ask the Congress to act. Much of this is legislation which I proposed in 1969, in 1970, and to the first session of this Ninety-second Congress last year, and on which I feel it is essential that action be completed this year.

I am not presenting proposals which have attractive labels but no hope of passage. I am presenting only vital programs which are within the capacity of the Congress to enact, within the capacity of the budget to finance, and which I believe should be above partisanship—programs which deal with urgent priorities for the nation, which should and must be the subject of bipartisan action by this Congress in the interests of the country in 1972.

When I took the oath of office on the steps of this building just three years ago today, the nation was ending one of the most tortured decades in its history.

The 1960s were a time of great progress in many areas. They were also a time of great agony—the agonies of war, of inflation, of rapidly rising crime, of deteriorating cities—of hopes raised and disappointed, and of anger and frustration that led finally to violence, and to the worst civil discord in a century.

To recall these troubles is not to point fingers of blame. The nation was so torn in those final years of the sixties that many in both parties questioned whether America could be governed at all.

The nation has made significant progress in these first years of the seventies.

Our cities are no longer engulfed by civil disorders.

Our colleges and universities have again become places of learning instead of battlegrounds.

A beginning has been made on preserving and protecting our environment.

The rate of increase in crime has been slowed—and here in the District of Columbia, the one city where the Federal Government has direct jurisdiction, serious crime in 1971 was actually reduced by 13 percent from the year before.

Most important—because of the beginnings that have been made, we can say today that the year 1972 can be the year in which America may make the greatest progress in twenty-five years toward achieving our goal of being at peace with all the nations in the world.

As our involvement in the war in Vietnam comes to an end, we must now go on to build a generation of peace.

To achieve that goal, we must face realistically the need to maintain our defenses.

In the past three years, we have reduced the burden of arms. For the first time in twenty years, spending on defense has been brought below spending on human resources.

As we look to the future, we find encouraging progress in our negotiations with the Soviet Union on limitation of strategic arms. Looking further into the future, we hope there can eventually be agreement on the mutual reduction of arms. But until there is such a mutual agreement, we must maintain the strength necessary to deter war.

Because of rising research and development costs, because of increases in military and civilian pay, and because of the need to proceed with new weapons systems, my budget for the coming fiscal year will provide for an increase in defense spending.

Strong military defenses are not the enemy of peace. They are the guardian of peace.

There could be no more misguided set of priorities than one which would tempt others by weakening America, and thereby endanger the peace of the world.

In our foreign policies, we have entered a new era. The world has changed greatly in the eleven years since President John F. Kennedy said, in his Inaugural Address, "We shall pay any price, bear any burden, meet any hardship, support any friend, oppose any foe, to assure the survival and the success of liberty."

Our policy has been carefully and deliberately adjusted to meet the new realities of the new world we now live in.

We make only those commitments we are able and prepared to meet.

Our commitment to freedom remains strong and unshakable. But others must bear their share of the burden of defending freedom around the world.

This is our policy:

> We will maintain a nuclear deterrent adequate to meet any threat to the security of the United States or of our allies.
>
> We will help other nations develop the capability of defending themselves.
>
> We will faithfully honor all of our treaty commitments.

We will act to defend our interests whenever and wherever they are threatened any place in the world. But where our interests or our treaty commitments are not involved our role will be limited.

We will not intervene militarily.

But we will use our influence to prevent war.

If war comes we will use our influence to try to stop it.

Once war is over we will do our share in helping to bind up the wounds of those who have participated in it.

I shall soon be visiting the People's Republic of China and the Soviet Union. I shall go there with no illusions. We have great differences with both powers. We will continue to have great differences. But peace depends on the ability of great powers to live together on the same planet despite their differences. We would not be true to our obligation to generations yet unborn if we failed to seize this moment to do everything in our power to insure that we will be able to talk about these differences rather than fight about them.

As we look back over this century, we can be proud of our nation's record in foreign affairs.

America has given more generously of itself toward maintaining freedom, preserving peace and alleviating human suffering around the globe than any nation has ever done.

We have fought four wars in this century—but our power has never been used to break the peace, only to keep it; never to destroy freedom, only to defend it. We now have within our reach the goal of ensuring that the next generation can be the first generation in this century to be spared the scourges of war.

Here at home, we are making progress toward our goal of a new prosperity without war.

Industrial production, consumer spending, retail sales and personal income all have been rising. Total employment and real income are the highest in history. New home-building starts this past year reached the highest level ever. Business and consumer confidence have both been rising. Interest rates are down, and the rate of inflation is down. We can look with confidence to 1972 as the year when the back of inflation will finally be broken.

Good as this record is, it is not good enough—not when we still have an unemployment rate of 6 percent.

It is not enough to point out that this was the rate of the early, peacetime years of the 1960s, or that, if the more than two million men released from the Armed Forces and defense-related industries were still on their wartime jobs, unemployment would be far lower.

Our goal is full employment in peacetime—and we intend to meet that goal.

The Congress has helped to meet it by passing our job-creating tax program last month.

The historic monetary agreements we have reached with the major European nations, Canada and Japan will help meet it, by providing new markets for American products—and thus new jobs for American workers.

Our budget will help meet it, by being expansionary without being inflationary—a job-producing budget that will help take up the gap as the economy expands to full employment.

Our program to raise farm income will help meet it, by helping to revitalize rural America—and by giving to America's farmers their fair share of America's productivity.

We will also help meet our goal of full employment in peacetime with a set of major initiatives to stimulate more imaginative use of America's great capacity for technological advance, and to direct it toward improving the quality of life for every American.

In reaching the moon, we saw what miracles American technology is capable of achieving. Now the time has come to move more deliberately toward making full use of that technology here on earth, in harnessing the wonders of science to the service of man.

I shall soon send to the Congress a special message proposing a new program of Federal partnership in technological research and development—with Federal incentives to increase private research, and federally-supported research on projects designed to improve our everyday lives in ways that will range from improving mass transit to developing new systems of emergency health care that could save thousands of lives annually.

Historically, our superior technology and high productivity have made it possible for America's workers to be the most highly paid in the world, and for our goods still to compete in world markets.

Now that other nations are moving rapidly forward in technology, the answer to the new competition is not to build a wall around America, but rather to remain competitive by improving our own technology still further, and by increasing productivity in American industry.

Our new monetary and trade agreements will make it possible for American goods to compete fairly in the world's markets—but they still must compete. The new technology program will not only put to use the skills of many highly-trained Americans—skills that might otherwise be wasted. It will also help meet the growing technological challenge from abroad, and thus help to create new industries as well as creating more jobs for America's workers in producing for the world's markets.

This second session of the Ninety-second Congress already has before it more than ninety major Administration proposals which still await action.

I have discussed these in the written message that I delivered today.

They include our programs to improve life for the aging; to combat crime and drug abuse; to improve health services and to ensure that no one will be denied needed health care because of inability to pay; to protect workers' pension rights; to promote equal opportunity for members of minorities and others who have been left behind; to expand consumer protection; to improve the environment; to revitalize rural America; to help the cities; to launch new initiatives in education; to improve transportation, and to put an end to costly labor tie-ups in transportation.

They also include basic reforms which are essential if our structure of Government is to be adequate to the needs of the decades ahead.

They include reform of our wasteful and outmoded welfare system—and substitution of a new system that provides work requirements and work incentives for those who can help themselves, income support for those who cannot help themselves, and fairness for the working poor.

They include a $17.6 billion program of Federal revenue sharing with the states and localities—as an investment in their renewal, and an investment of faith in the people.

They also include a sweeping reorganization of the executive branch of the Federal Government, so that it will be more efficient, more responsive, and able to meet the challenges of the decades ahead.

One year ago, I laid before the opening session of this Congress six great goals.

One of these was welfare reform. That proposal has been before the Congress now for nearly two and a half years.

My proposals on revenue sharing, Government reorganization, health care and the environment have now been before the Congress for nearly a year. Many of my other major proposals have been here as long or longer.

Nineteen seventy-one was a year of consideration of these measures. Now let us join in making 1972 a year of action on them—action by the Congress, for the nation and for the people of America.

In addition, there is one pressing need which I have not previously covered, but which must be placed on the national agenda.

We long have looked to the local property tax as the main source of financing for public primary and secondary education.

As a result, soaring school costs and soaring property tax rates now threaten both our communities and our schools. They threaten communities because property taxes—which more than doubled in the ten years from 1960 to 1970—have become one of the most oppressive and discriminatory of all taxes, hitting most cruelly at the elderly and the retired; and they threaten schools, as hard-pressed voters understandably reject new bond issues at the polls.

The problem has been given even greater urgency by three recent court decisions, which have held the conventional method of financing schools through local property taxes discriminatory and unconstitutional.

Nearly two years ago, I named a special presidential commission to study the problems of school finance; and I also directed the Federal departments to look into the same problems. We are developing comprehensive proposals to meet these problems.

This issue involves two complex and interrelated sets of problems: support of the schools, and the basic relationships of Federal, state and local governments in any tax reforms.

Under the leadership of the Secretary of the Treasury, we are carefully reviewing the tax aspects; and I have this week enlisted the Advisory Commission on Intergovernmental Relations in addressing the intergovernmental relations aspects.

I have asked this bipartisan commission to review our proposals for Federal action to cope with the gathering crisis of school finance and property taxes. Later in the year, when both commissions have completed their studies, I shall make my final recommendations for relieving the burden of property taxes and providing both fair and adequate financing for our children's education.

All of my recommendations, however, will be rooted in one fundamental principle with which there can be no compromise: local school boards must have control over local schools.

As we look ahead over the coming decades, vast new growth and change are not only certainties. They will be the dominant reality of our life in America.

Surveying the certainty of rapid change, we can be like a fallen rider caught in the stirrups—or we can sit high in the saddle, the masters of change, directing it on a course that we choose.

The secret of mastering change in today's world is to reach back to old and proven principles, and to adapt them, with imagination and intelligence, to the new realities of a new age.

This is what we have done in the proposals that I have laid before the Congress. They are rooted in basic principles that are as enduring as human nature and as robust as the American experience; and they are responsive to new conditions. Thus they represent a spirit of change that is really renewal.

As we look back to these old principles, we find them as timely as they are timeless.

We believe in independence, and self-reliance, and in the creative value of the competitive spirit.

We believe in full and equal opportunity for all Americans, and in the protection of individual rights and liberties.

We believe in the family as the keystone of the community, and in the community as the keystone of the nation.

We believe in compassion toward those in need.

We believe in a system of law, justice and order as the basis of a genuinely free society.

We believe that a person should get what he works for —and those who can should work for what they get.

We believe in the capacity of people to make their own decisions, in their own lives and in their own communities— and we believe in their right to make those decisions.

In applying these principles, we have done so with a full understanding that our quest in the seventies is not merely for more, but for better—for a better quality of life for all Americans.

Thus, for example, we are giving a new measure of attention to cleaning up our air and water, and to making our surroundings more attractive. Thus we are providing broader support for the arts, and helping stimulate a deeper appreciation of what they can contribute to the nation's activities and to our individual lives.

Nothing matters more to the quality of our lives than the way we treat one another—than our capacity to live respectfully together as a unified society, with a full and generous regard for the rights of others and the feelings of others.

As we recover from the turmoil and violence of recent years, as we learn once again to speak with one another instead of shouting at one another, we are regaining that capacity.

As is customary here, on this occasion, I have been talking about programs. These programs are important. But even more important than programs is what we *are* as a nation—what we mean as a nation, to ourselves and to the world.

In New York harbor stands one of the most famous statues in the world—the Statue of Liberty, the gift in 1886 of the people of France to the people of the United States. This statue is more than a landmark; it is a symbol—a symbol of what America has meant to the world.

It reminds us that what America has meant is not its wealth, not its power, but its spirit and purpose—a land that enshrines liberty and opportunity, and that has held out a hand of welcome to millions in search of a better and a fuller and above all, a freer life.

The world's hopes poured into America, along with its people—and those hopes, those dreams, that have been brought from every corner of the world, have become a part of the hope that we hold out to the world.

Four years from now, America will celebrate the 200th anniversary of its founding as a nation.

There are some who say that the old Spirit of '76 is dead —that we no longer have the strength of character, the idealism, the faith in our founding purposes, that that spirit represents.

Those who say this do not know America.

We have been undergoing self-doubts and self-criticism. But these are the other side of our growing sensitivity to the persistence of want in the midst of plenty, and of our impatience with the slowness with which age-old ills are being overcome.

If we were indifferent to the shortcomings of our society, or complacent about our institutions, or blind to the lingering inequities—then we would have lost our way.

The fact that we have these concerns is evidence that our ideals are still strong: And indeed, they remind us that what is best about America is its compassion. They remind us that in the final analysis, America is great not because it is strong, not because it is rich, but because it is good.

Let us reject the narrow visions of those who would tell us that we are evil because we are not yet perfect, that we are corrupt because we are not yet pure, that all the sweat and toil and sacrifice that have gone into the building of America were for naught because the building is not yet done.

Let us see that the path we are traveling is wide, with room in it for all of us, and that its direction is toward a better nation in a more peaceful world.

Never has it mattered more that we go forward together.

The leadership of America is here today, in this chamber —the Supreme Court, the Cabinet, the Senate, the House of Representatives.

Together, we hold the future of the nation, and the conscience of the nation, in our hands.

Because this year is an election year, it will be a time of great pressure.

If we yield to that pressure, and fail to deal seriously with the historic challenges that we face, then we will have failed America. We will have failed the trust of millions of

Americans, and shaken the confidence they have a right to place in their Government.

Never has a Congress had a greater opportunity to leave a legacy of profound and constructive reform for the nation than this Congress.

If we succeed in these tasks, there will be credit enough for all—not only for doing what is right, but for doing it in the right way, by rising above partisan interest to serve the national interest.

If we fail, then more than any of us, America will be the loser.

That is why my call upon the Congress today is for a high statesmanship—so that in the years to come, Americans will look back and say that because it withstood the intense pressures of a political year, and achieved such great good for the American people, and for the future of this nation—this was truly a great Congress.

ECONOMIC INJUSTICE IN AMERICA TODAY [3]

SHIRLEY CHISHOLM [4]

The determination of Representative Shirley Chisholm (Democrat, New York) to campaign for the Democratic nomination for the presidency was an indication of growing black power. Popular among feminists and college groups, the former schoolteacher would not be deterred from entering the race. She told an audience at the University of Tennessee on February 2, 1972: "I am very concerned about man's inhumanity to man. Because I am a woman, because I am black, I, Shirley Chisholm, am a part of these two segments, and I will lead the women into the political arena to preserve our most important resource—our people." Although blacks were divided over whether to support her and almost no one thought that she could command much strength at the national convention, Mrs. Chisholm won respect and admiration from many Americans for her perseverance, determination, and straight talk. She is likely to remain a significant personality for the seventies.

Norman C. Miller of the *Wall Street Journal* (February 14, 1972) explains her position as follows: "She projects herself as a leader of a coalition of have-nots—including blacks and women but also students, Indians and Mexican-Americans (whom she addresses in fluent Spanish). These groups must combine, she says, to elect a bloc of convention delegates who will vote only for a candidate who agrees to their 'non-negotiable demands.'"

A speech that Mrs. Chisholm delivered to the students of the Newark College of Engineering, April 15, 1972 clearly shows how she presented this message to students. Her bluntness enabled her to reach her student listeners. Nan Robertson in the New York *Times* (February 14, 1972) described the black congresswoman as a "commanding and imperious presence, holding herself like a queen with her back as straight as a ruler. Her syntax and delivery are flawless in her extemporaneous speeches." She demonstrated that she is an effective campaigner, and is able to stir enthusiasm outside of New York. Persons interested in another aspect of the congresswoman should read her speech "It Is Time to Reassess Our National Priorities," reprinted in REPRESENTATIVE AMERICAN SPEECHES: 1968-1969, pages 68-72.

[3] Delivered to the Newark College of Engineering, Newark, N.J., April 15, 1972.

[4] For biographical note, see Appendix.

Political participation has been and continues to be the way individuals gain access to Government in this country. But . . . there has been a failure in the process of political participation—we all know this—and I think most of us are now aware that the failure has done its damage in Government, so that individuals in this country now feel powerless and out of control of their own lives. We have a Government that is remote. We have a Government that is responsive to other institutions that are equally remote: large corporations, conglomerates, powerful interest groups, and an uncaring or condescending financial establishment. We have a Government that has, in short, lost its credibility.

There are a lot of theories about why this Government of ours has lost touch with its own people. But if we were to wait until we had a total agreement about exactly what is wrong to try to make changes, we could all be sitting here for two or three centuries and we would still probably be without answers, no changes would have been made, and the problems would be worse.

We don't have time to sit and wait. We have to make an input. This is why you see me here in New Jersey today—a black woman from Brooklyn, New York—as a candidate for nomination to the United States presidency.

I have my own theory about what we can do to improve this United States Government. And my theory is easy to understand. We have to expand the base of political participation in this country so that the decisions made reflect the thinking of more than just a small segment of the population. For I believe that you *cannot* exclude over one half of the population—women—and one tenth of the population—black people—and exclude in addition the points of view represented by young people, poor people, the Spanish-speaking and other minorities—you cannot exclude all of these groups from influence over governmental decisions and social policy without finding that the Government is out of touch and that its policy is narrow and damaging to the majority of people it is intended to serve.

Let's take the American economy for an example of what I mean by "narrow and damaging" policy. Today, we have no economic bill of rights, and we need one. We must re-negotiate the basic terms of our economic relationships in this society.

The American Indian knows that the capital he needs to start basic economic development in Indian communities is not available in significant amounts through public agencies of Government, yet he knows that without that capital he will continue to be exploited on and near reservations, in urban centers, and wherever he lives.

Ask him and he will tell you that the American economy denies his citizenship.

Ask the Chicano in East Los Angeles, in which 35 percent of the housing is substandard, whether President Nixon's announcement of a record 2 million housing starts in 1971 had anything to do with improvement of housing in East Los Angeles.

Or talk to the Spanish-speaking migrant worker in California, or Texas, about the abundance of good health and medical care which this Administration proclaims: That migrant worker knows that infant and maternal mortality among his or her people is 125 percent higher than the national rate; that influenza and pneumonia death rates are 200 percent higher than the national rate; that death from tuberculosis and infectious disease is 260 percent higher: And life expectancy itself for the migrant worker is 49 years—compared with 67.5 years for the members of the silent majority.

Talk to the young black man or woman in our urban areas.

In urban poverty neighborhoods the unemployment rate three years ago was almost 6 percent—on the average—and that is the figure which today the President's economic policies have bestowed on the entire nation—on the average. Yet today in the urban black ghetto unemployment averages 12 percent and rising! Is that where President Nixon plans to take the nation during the next four years? He has made this entire nation an unemployment disaster area comparable to conditions which existed only in ghettos three years ago.

In the city of Seattle the Nixon economic policy has created a whole new class of involuntary poor—middle-class Americans who five years ago never thought they would have to know what the bitter sting and emptiness of unemployment feels like.

I mention the systematic exclusion of the Indian, the Chicano, and the ghetto black from the American economy only as examples of a much broader and more disturbing pattern.

They are not the only ones who live outside the system. Children under sixteen comprise 38 percent of the poor; and households headed by persons aged sixty-five and older make up 23 percent of all the poor in America today. Women, regardless of race or class, find themselves the victims of economic discrimination so consistently on the basis of their sex alone that they are uniting across a broad front to fight for basic economic equality.

The coalition women have formed—in which the white college graduate links arms with the black household domestic worker whose only education may be life itself—is the beginning of the union of the disenfranchised peoples of America. As the American labor movement discovered years ago there is no better or quicker way to bring people together than the common experience of economic injustice!

Economic injustice, however, is now no longer the exclusive possession of the poor.

A union of the disenfranchised, a coalition of those who are on the outside of the American economy, will not be purely a union of racial minorities, the young, and women. For economic injustice has shown its ugly head in millions of American homes where five years ago it was unknown.

If unemployment is not enough, there is the question of interest rates on home loans, the price of food and clothing, the price of gasoline and heating oil, and the ever-increasing cost of everyday public transportation in city after city.

The Administration's sensational price control program, in the face of repeated and categorical statements by the President that he would never use such controls, was at best an effort to close the barn door after the horse of runaway inflation had long gone. In fact, the door was never even half closed.

I have been particularly concerned about the rent control aspect of Phase II. The rent controls were highly publicized by the Administration—so highly publicized in fact that they amounted to an open season on tenants by landlords who declared that the President had said, "Now is the time for a rent increase, so get it while you can."

Or look at food prices now that we're into Phase II. The Consumer Price Index for food showed an increase of four tenths of a percent in December after the conclusion of Phase I controls: The December figure, according to a recent article entitled "Higher Prices Ahead for Groceries" in *U.S. News & World Report,* translates into a 4.8 percent annual increase in food prices—double the rate which occurred under Phase I.

And in some notable specific items, food prices skyrocketed immediately after the end of Phase I: tomatoes up 50 percent a pound from 43 cents to 60 cents on the average; lettuce per head up from 34 to 47 cents, an increase of 38 percent. Across the board, the cost of food in grocery stores went up 1.3 percent in December, twice what is usual for that month.

And Dr. Herbert Stein, chairman of the President's Council of Economic Advisers states that he wouldn't be surprised if the "bulge" in prices would *increase* in the future. He did not mention the increases in other areas as well—the cost of new cars and gasoline during December for one.

The cost of living is first on all of our minds this important year. Yet the President has decided that it is a year for travel.

But I ask—when is he going to make a "Trip to Peking" in regard to the basic problems facing us in the United States this year? He is willing to go halfway 'round the world—yet he doesn't have time to walk ten blocks from the White House in Washington and look at the lives people are living under Phase II.

While the President was in Peking, almost 21 million Americans over sixty-five—roughly 10 percent of our population—faced the rising costs of food and services with fixed incomes—fixed at a median of $2,800 a year if you are an old man, fixed at $1,400 a year if you happen to be an old woman. The most recent survey—published in 1970—showed that 90 percent of these citizens over sixty-five subsist on retirement benefits of which the bulk is Social Security payments.

In the President's State of the Union Message January 20 of this year he laid special emphasis on "action for the aging" and urged Congress to enact a 5 percent across-the-board increase in Social Security. That my friends is just two tenths of a percent above the 4.8 percent increase in food prices we are now experiencing in Phase II.

And I think it is very significant that President Nixon lied to the American people when he spoke to the nation on January 20 and said that "our program of wage and price controls is working," and cited as evidence for that statement the fact that the Consumer Price Index, and I quote him again, ". . . which rose at a yearly rate of slightly over 6 percent during 1969 and the first half of 1970, rose at a rate of only 1.7 percent from August through November of 1971."

The next day, January 21, the White House released the figures which showed what the President deliberately omitted from his State of the Union Message: that during December 1971 and into the month of January consumer prices rose by 4.8 percent, well on their way back to the previous outrageous levels.

Older Americans know what these figures mean. They mean taking scarce funds from this month's meager food budget and putting it into clothing if it's winter; or they mean less for medical care or medicine these months in order to buy food.

But since the President has decided this year to try to turn our attention to his foreign policy grandstanding, I would say a few words about the impact of international economic decisions as they affect you and me.

Our economic bill of rights should set forth certain basic principles regarding foreign economic policy. If I am elected President, one of the first acts of my Administration would be high-level reconsideration of the relation between our international economic decisions and their impact, in particular, on the poor people of America.

Every day the President virtually by himself makes decisions on foreign trade, surcharges, tariffs, and balance of payments which have direct consequences on the lives of millions of Americans, but neither the Congress nor the American public share in a great many of those decisions.

As part of the President's Annual Economic Report, I would submit to the Congress an "Economic Impact Statement" similar to the environmental impact statements required now under Federal law. The Economic Impact Statement would show how, for example, foreign trade quotas or changes in tariff rates impact on various groups in our national economy at home. Today this is not done. President Nixon acts on the assumption that what is good for the international bankers and corporations on Wall Street will inevitably trickle down to the middle-class consumer and the unemployed person.

Yet the only things trickling down from this Administration are taxes and increased costs of goods and services.

Take for example the so-called value-added tax which the Nixon economists are now promoting. It is nothing other than a thinly disguised sales tax on a national level, designed to add taxes at each stage of the journey from manufacturer (or importer) to the consumer.

Now in theory, says the President, this spreads the tax load on that item and indeed it would if rigid price controls existed at the retail level, so that the item could not be increased in cost along the way. But what do you think will really happen? The pattern under Phase II is that *costs*, not savings, are being passed along to the consumer.

A sales tax is the enemy of the poor person. It is the enemy of the elderly couple who live on fixed income. And it is the enemy of the everyday American consumer, poor or not.

I am completely opposed to increasing the debt ceiling without basic tax reform. What we need in this country today is leadership which has the courage to call for *income tax reform* to put the burden where it must be placed, on those who can afford to pay.

It makes me sick to read every year the "honor roll" of all the wealthy Americans who avoided paying income taxes this year or last because of loopholes and special subsidies. Yet in the face of chronic and continuing inequities, the Administration suggests raising the debt ceiling while creating the value-added tax to bring in new revenues from the people at the bottom of the economic ladder.

I say the time to force tax reform is now, and the way to force it is to keep the lid on the debt ceiling and end the system of special privilege which *is* the tax system of this country today.

The American people don't need college degrees to understand the phony arithmetic of the Nixon economy. In 1971, individual citizen taxpayers paid in $86.2 billion in taxes, while corporations—which control 90 percent of the wealth of this nation—paid in $26.8 billion in income taxes.

In other words, you and I collectively paid in roughly $60 billion more than all the great corporations of this country.

Well, where did President Nixon put that money? He spent $77.6 billion on national defense, $3.5 billion on outer space, almost $20 billion on interest to pay off previous extensions of the debt limit, $12 billion on commerce and transportation, and about $20 billion on programs which are designed to help people get on their feet in our economy.

In the national defense budget, just under $19 billion was spent on procurement of hardware in 1971—in short, the corporations did not quite break even, they took a $7 billion loss in the speculative market on paying income taxes to the Federal Government. Of course, the corporations actually got back considerably more than the $26.8 billion they paid in taxes, when you look at the money in every sector of the budget which goes not to the citizen but to private producers of Government services.

In the last year we have seen a whole series of incredible Government welfare subsidies for the huge corporations: the supersonic transport, the C-5A giant aircraft, and most recently the President's endorsement of a multibillion expenditure on the space shuttle. A space shuttle to where? Mars, Jupiter, or Saturn?

I know a lot of Americans who would be glad to settle for better bus service from their home to their jobs, or from poor neighborhoods to areas of the city where jobs are to be found. Repeated studies of riots in urban ghettos show that lack of adequate transportation was a big factor in the discontent and bitterness which caused riot conditions to erupt, but President Nixon's answer is to build a space shuttle or an SST with precious public funds, to serve a tiny elite of the population or to stimulate the economy of a state or region by creating massive and useless technological public-works projects.

Why don't we get this country to work again at things which need to be done?

I would start with the construction and maintenance of a good subway system in every city over 250,000 population. Our city streets and basic public facilities are badly dilapidated in huge areas of inner cities—even in suburban areas for that matter: many cities have no public sidewalks, bad street lighting, poorly maintained public parks. And perhaps

one of the biggest items of unfinished business is the rehabilitation of existing housing—this in itself would be a prime
stimulus to the revitalization of our basic economy and job
market.

I am fully aware that there are important aspects of the
economy which are served by technological industry. For
example, in Japan the best engineers and scientists perfected
high-speed rail transportation which could be a model for
this country. But we waste our best minds on outer space!
And our slow train service between major cities is a disgrace
to a society which thinks of itself as the most technologically
advanced in the world.

We have come to the point where we have allowed our
economic well-being to wither away and rot in order to support a few highly specialized and remote kinds of activity,
much of it defense-oriented.

The price you and I have paid is not necessarily better
protection at home or less involvement in foreign and distant
wars, as the availability of this hardware seems to often beg
for its use: The real price we pay is in shoddy consumer
goods, rotting cities which can no longer pay their share of
taxes, increased property taxes in suburban areas to pay for
the declining revenue base in the older parts of cities, and
collapse of school systems because taxpayers revolt and say
they have had enough. And the basic reason, the underlying
cause, of this cycle is the fundamental lack of balance in
national priorities. If the priorities were set by the people
for a change, some of this imbalance would be removed.

WOMEN'S POLITICAL POWER

A NEW KIND OF SOUTHERN STRATEGY [1]

BELLA S. ABZUG [2]

The women's liberation movement has made rapid strides during the past year. Now in the field are such organizations as the National Organization for Women, the Women's League Defense Fund, and Women's Equity Action League. In July 1971, the National Women's Political Caucus made its appearance in Washington, D. C., under the guidance of Representatives Bella S. Abzug and Shirley Chisholm (Democrats, New York), and Ms. Betty Friedan.

One of the most striking personalities among women speakers is Bella Abzug, Representative from the Nineteenth Congressional District in Manhattan and the first Jewish woman to win a seat in Congress. Inspiring such epithets as "Battling Bella," "Hurricane Bella," "Mother Courage," "the Wicked Witch," and "Bellacose Abzug," the New York congresswoman has long been a passionate crusader for women's liberation, minority rights, and the antiwar movement. She is described as "flamboyant, fearless," "truculent and courageous," "loud, good-natured, plain-talking and seemingly indestructible," and as "one of the most vividly colorful political personalities New York has ever produced."

Current Biography (1971) describes her as follows: "Broadshouldered, husky-looking . . . often described by reporters as 'chunky.' She has brown eyes and short reddish-brown hair, and her large collection of wide-brimmed hats has become a trademark." She has what has been called "a raspy, Bronx-accented voice." Her delivery is direct, enthusiastic, and forceful. Her language, often earthy, is plain but meaningful. Not easily intimidated, she understands how to win her way with most audiences.

The speech given here is one that Representative Abzug delivered at the Southern Women's Conference on Education for Delegate Selection, a two-day conference, February 11 and 12, held at Scarritt College in Nashville, Tennessee, under the leadership

---

[1] Delivered to Southern Women's Conference on Education for Delegate Selection, Scarritt College, Nashville, Tennessee, February 12, 1972. Quoted by permission.

[2] For biographical note, see Appendix.

of the Women's Political Caucus. Her listeners were 357 women coming from the twelve southern states, a preponderance from the Democratic party. In this speech her goal was to stir her listeners to challenge the rules and procedures under which delegates to the presidential nominating conventions are chosen.

One of her listeners (Ms. Roberta Madden) reacted to Bella Abzug's speech as perhaps many of her listeners at Nashville did:

> Speaking boldly and confidently, in her husky New York-accented voice, Ms. Abzug acknowledged the "conscious unity" among women everywhere in the country today, a feeling of unity that became almost palpable as she spoke. . . . Looking at her as she stood on the small stage, at the broad-brimmed hat she wears as a trademark, at her strong, sure hands gesturing as she talked, I recognized this solid, sensible, beautifully human woman as *my* representative. "Yes!" I kept thinking all the while, "*that's* what *I've* been trying to say!"

As cochairwoman of the National Women's Political Caucus, I welcome you to the women's political power movement.

I am not an authority on the South, but I suspect that this is the first time a conference such as this has ever been held here. You are making history today.

You are creating a new kind of "southern strategy" for 1972 . . . a political strategy for women who have been shut out of power and who are determined that this is the year to win full citizenship and participation in political decision making for the women of the South—white and black.

As you come together here to study the techniques of electoral politics, you are part of a nationwide movement. You are doing what women all across the country are doing, and I predict that the male politicians are in for some real surprises in this election year. Reports are coming in of women turning out in unexpectedly large numbers at political meetings—not just the big rallies, but the small precinct meetings where the political process starts. And I hear that the women are asking sharp questions of the candidates and they're not satisfied with platitudes or with having their babies kissed.

I think we can take some credit for that. We've been doing a lot of political consciousness-raising. Since the National Women's Political Caucus was organized in Washington last July, women have organized caucuses in more than forty states, North, South, East and West—and they're learning fast.

Our women are as diverse as America itself, as diverse as you who have come here today. Women who are young and old, rich and poor, white, black, Chicanas, Puerto Ricans and Indians, women who come from all parties and no parties, women who are in the United States Congress and women who have never held office.

Your presence here indicates the conscious unity that binds you together with thousands of women across the country and the sense of common wrongs and injustices that exists among millions of women, whether they work in universities, factories, offices or in the home.

We are women with many different life styles. Television and the other media which thrive on the offbeat and the sensational have tried to depict the women's liberation movement as an assembly of bra-burning, neurotic, man-hating exhibitionists. Don't let them fool you.

I have been to hundreds of women's meetings and I have yet to see a bra burned.

But I have met and talked to women who were burning with indignation at the wastefulness and stupidity of a society that makes second-class citizens of half its population.

Women, in fact, are 53 percent of the electorate. Yet throughout our history and now, more than a half century after we won the vote, women are still almost invisible in government, in elected posts, in high administrative decision-making positions, in the judiciary.

We are determined to change that. And we intend to do it by organizing ourselves and by reaching out to women everywhere.

I would like to read to you from the Statement of Purpose adopted by the National Women's Political Caucus at its founding meeting. It addressed its appeal to:

. . . every woman whose abilities have been wasted by the second-class, subservient, underpaid, or powerless positions to which female human beings are consigned

To every woman who sits at home with little control over her own life, much less the powerful institutions of the country, wondering if there isn't more to life than this

To every woman who must go on welfare because, even when she can get a job, she makes about half the money paid to a man for the same work

To every minority woman who has endured the stigma of being twice-different from the white male ruling class

To every woman who has experienced the ridicule or hostility reserved by this country—and often by its political leaders—for women who dare to express the hopes and ambitions that are natural to every human being

To all these women—and they are nearly all of us—we said that it is time for us to join together to act against the sexism, racism, institutional violence and poverty that disfigure our beautiful land.

We said it is time that women organize to get an equal share of representation and power in the political structures of government.

It is time that we organize to see that women's issues, the priorities of life, not war, are taken seriously and become the policy of government, a government that represents us.

Wherever I go, and I have traveled a great deal in the past year, I have found a strong community of interest among huge numbers of American women, a strong commitment to changing the direction of our society.

Women are in the forefront of the peace movement, the civil rights and equal rights movement, the environment and consumer movements, the child care movement. This is part of your tradition too. It was southern ladies who organized the Committee to Stop Lynching here in the South many years ago, and it was a woman who sat in the *front* of a bus in Montgomery, Alabama, and made history.

Just a few weeks ago I sat in Congress and heard the President give the State of the Union address. There were more than seven hundred of us seated on the main floor of the House. You may have heard the President say, Here we have assembled the Government of the United States, the members of the House, the Senate, the Supreme Court, the Cabinet.

I looked around and of these 700 leaders of Government, there were just 12 women. Could anything be more disgraceful? Eleven women out of 435 members of the House. One woman out of 100 in the Senate. No women in the Cabinet. No women on the Supreme Court, although the President has had four separate opportunities to appoint one.

In fact, there were more women up in the balcony than on the floor, and as onlookers their role was to look pretty, to applaud dutifully and to be silent.

But we have come to the end of silence. There is too much to say. The men haven't done such a great job by themselves. Women look at a nation run by a male executive branch, a male Congress, male governors and legislatures, a male Pentagon, and male corporations and banks, and they rightly ask:

If we shared equally with men the authority of government, would we condone the spending of more than a trillion dollars in the past twenty-five years for killing and useless weapons—

when our cities are dying of neglect

when families go hungry in Appalachia

when children in South Carolina suffer from malnutrition and are afflicted with worms

when people live in shacks or are forced to go on welfare because there are no jobs for them

when there are not enough hospitals, doctors and schools

when our young people are becoming more and more alienated from a society they regard as without soul or purpose

I think not.

I believe that shutting women out of political power and decision-making roles has resulted in a terrible mutilation of our society. It is at least partly responsible for our present crisis of lopsided priorities and distorted values. It is responsible too for the masculine mystique, the obsession with militarism that has made the nuclear missile the symbol of American power and that equates our national honor with continuing the senseless killing in Indochina, continuing a war which American women—in even larger numbers than men—say must be ended.

As you know, some of the most powerful men in the House are from the South. They hold the leadership posts. They head the most important committees—Armed Services, Appropriations, Ways and Means, and others. They are the ones who decide whether we are to build more bombs or more schools. They are there because of the seniority system and because they are reelected year after year without any significant opposition. Women help elect these men, and then men use their power to deny women their most basic needs.

I hope that this is the year when some of you women will begin to challenge these men and put them on notice that they don't have a lifetime hold on those congressional seats.

Don't get me wrong. I am not saying that the men in Congress are totally indifferent to the needs of women. Many are genuinely concerned. Others are catching on to the fact that they had better be concerned, and still others are now pretending to care.

But it is also a fact of life that it is the victim of discrimination who feels most deeply the injustice of discrimination and who is most determined to end it.

Consider what is happening in Congress in connection with the Equal Employment Opportunities Commission. A filibuster in the Senate has just defeated an attempt to equip the EEOC with effective cease-and-desist power to stop employers from discriminating against women, blacks and other minorities. We lost the same fight in the House, too.

The shameful facts of discrimination against black people have been set before the nation, but I wonder how many are fully aware of the scandalous and all-pervasive discrimination against women of all colors.

Do you know that women now make up 37 percent of the labor force . . . that almost thirty million women work, most of them because they need the money . . . that seven out of ten work at menial clerical jobs, and most of the others at service or factory jobs?

Do you know that only 7 percent of doctors are women, earn less than $5,000 a year? Do you know that even when they are better educated than men, they wind up with worse jobs . . . that even when they perform the same work as men, they usually get paid less, and that promotions usually go to men, not women?

Do you know that only 7 percent of doctors are women, and that we have only a toehold in the other professions? Do you know that the number of women in college and university teaching is actually declining?

Do you know about the 4.5 million mothers in the labor force who have youngsters under six? Nearly 6 million pre-school children whose mothers have to work to help buy their food and clothing, but in all of this great land we have only enough child care centers to accommodate a half million children. And when we finally passed a child care act at this last session, the President vetoed it. He said it was fiscally irresponsible, and yet a few weeks later he asked for twice as much money—$4 billion—to increase military spending. And he also vetoed it because he said it was a threat to family life!

I would suggest that women are greater authorities on family life than is the President. It is they who bear the children and raise them, many as heads of the family. It is they who work as waitresses, secretaries, hospital aides, factory hands, and in the fields. And it is they who come home and have to clean and cook and care for their children and worry about getting baby sitters when they go to work the next day or night.

If we had more of these real experts in Congress, they would not let the President get away with pious invocations of a nonreal world. They would insist that instead of raising our military budget to $80 billion, as the President proposes, that we allocate money for child care centers, for training programs and more educational opportunities for women, for basic human needs.

And I believe that if we had a truly representative Congress, with at least half of its members women and with much greater representation of blacks and other minorities, we would get real, effective action to end discrimination. We would have not a filibuster, but an EEOC with teeth in it. We would have an Equal Rights Amendment.

I am not elevating women to sainthood, nor am I suggesting that all women share the same views, or that all women are good and all men are bad. But I do believe that because they have been excluded from political power for so long, they see with more clairvoyant eyes the deficiencies of our society. Their work in the voluntary organizations has made them the compassionate defenders of the victims of our distorted priorities. They know intimately the problems of the aged and the sick, of the neglected, miseducated child, the young soldiers returning home wounded in body or spirit.

There are only eleven of us women in the House. Some of us are Democrats, some Republicans, some liberals and some conservatives. But all of us supported the Mansfield Amendment which requires all American troops to be withdrawn from Indochina within six months. I find that very significant and an encouraging omen of things to come.

What is to come? Is this the year when women's political power will come of age? Or are we just going to make noise but no real progress?

I believe that in the seven months of our existence, the National Women's Political Caucus has already achieved a great deal.

As you know, in 1968 only 13 percent of the delegates to the Democratic convention were women. The Republicans did only slightly better, with 17 percent. Only 1 of the 180 delegations at both conventions was chaired by a woman.

This time we're going to do much, much better.

As standards for reasonable representation at the conventions, the women's caucus has voted that each state delegation should be comprised of no less than 50 percent women. It has also voted that racial minorities and young people should be present in each delegation in percentages at least as great as their percentage of the total state population.

We have set up task forces within the Caucus to meet with representatives of the Republican and Democratic parties to press the issue of representation. Our task force of Republican women is following up on this pledge. We do have a number of Republicans in the leadership of our caucus, including Elly Peterson, formerly head of the GOP's women's division, and Virginia Allen, who headed the President's Commission on the Status of Women. This is the commission that issued the report called *A Matter of Simple Justice,* which documented the pervasive discrimination against women in our society and made very specific proposals on how to end it. That report is gathering dust, and that is why Republican women find they have so much in common with the rest of us.

As for the Democratic party, it has a specific commitment to honor the guidelines of the McGovern-Fraser party reform commission which would ensure reasonable representation at the convention of women, youth and minorities. At a meeting which we held in Washington with Democratic Party Chairman Larry O'Brien and Patricia Harris, temporary chairman of the Credentials Committee (Carleen Waller was present, too), we obtained a definite statement that any delegation which does not contain at least 50 percent women and proportional representation of the young and minorities will be deemed in *prima facie* violation of the guidelines and subject to challenge.

We intend to hold the Democratic party leadership to that commitment. We are now engaged in a national effort to en-sure that at least half of the delegates are women, and we are prepared to challenge the credentials of delegations that are not representative.

So what you are doing today is part of an ongoing cam-paign for political recognition of women. You will find that the delegate selection process varies from state to state. It is highly complicated in some states and simple in others. Many of you have already found that out.

Learn the procedures, and go back to your states deter-mined to settle for nothing less than your full share. Whether they run on slates committed to specific candidates or to no candidate, women must join together at every stage of the delegation selection process—and form their own caucuses across slate lines to guarantee that women are not squeezed out, to make sure that male politicians don't try to use their wives or aunts as stand-ins and to agree on common goals and state their demands. They must do this at the precinct level, at the legislative district level, and at the state level. *We must be visible as women.*

Women will be wearing Muskie buttons, Humphrey but-tons, McGovern buttons, Lindsay buttons and I predict that a surprising number will be wearing Chisholm buttons. The more the better—because Shirley Chisholm's candidacy offers us one of the most effective ways to press our demands. But we are also going to be wearing *Womanpower—'72* buttons and ribbons because no matter what slates we're on, we're going to act together as women.

Let no one take us for granted.

I am recommending to the NWPC that on the opening day of the convention we cross slate lines and get women delegates to meet together, demonstrate our unified presence, and state our demands. We will serve notice that we want an equal share in leadership. We want a party and a platform actively committed to eradicating discrimination and making women first-class citizens in every aspect of their lives.

We want a party and a platform committed to working for a peaceful and humane society that meets the needs of all its people. And to make sure that this comes to pass, we want guarantees that women share equally in committee posts in the party and at the convention.

We want guarantees from the nominee, whoever he or she may be, that women will have an equal share in Government—an equal number of Cabinet posts and high administrative offices. And we want an end to the exclusion of women from the Supreme Court and their almost total exclusion from the lower courts.

We are prepared to use every means at our disposal to remove the "for men only" sign from American politics and to open wide our political institutions to women and to all underrepresented groups.

We intend to do this not only at the conventions, but in political contests all over the country. We will have more women running this year for local office, for the state legislature, for Congress. Some will run for the experience, and some will run to win. Some are already running. I have been getting phone calls from around the country. A woman is running for governor of Texas. Black women are running for Congress from Texas and California, and there are others who are planning to do so or who have already announced. At some point we're going to get all our women candidates together and introduce them to the nation.

We in the women's political movement have a responsibility to see that we do get some winners and that we pick out contests wisely. I would urge that in every state or region you get together, the sooner the better, and pick your concentration points. Choose your strongest candidates to run against the weakest incumbents. Try to select areas in which you can build coalitions with other underrepresented groups.

Remember, this is the year when the outs—all of us—are demanding "in."

Representatives of young people with a potential strength of twenty-five million new voters met in Chicago recently to organize a Youth Caucus, and they are now setting up caucuses in all the states. The black caucus is well organized, and other minority groups are also joining together to make their political power count.

I believe that with the organization of these groups we have the components of a New Majority—a majority of women, young people, minority groups and other Americans—small businessmen, working people, farmers, poor people—who share in our concerns and needs.

Working together, this New Majority has the capacity to change America, to lead us away from war and to work together instead for a society in which human needs are paramount, in which all people—men and women—who can work will have meaningful employment, in which women will have full citizenship and dignity as individuals, in which our children can learn and live free from the atmosphere of hatred and violence that has despoiled our land for so many years.

These are goals to which I believe most women will respond. What you do here this weekend at this historic first political meeting of southern womanpower will help create that kind of America.

SPEAKING FOR MINORITIES

SURVIVAL [1]

VERNON E. JORDAN, JR. [2]

Vernon E. Jordan, Jr., executive director of the National Urban League, has continued the program and emphasis of his great predecessor Whitney Young, Jr., who died so tragically in 1971 (see REPRESENTATIVE AMERICAN SPEECHES: 1970-1971). Mr. Jordan delivered at least three notable addresses during this last year: one at the Urban League Conference in Detroit (July 28, 1971); a second before the annual meeting of the Cleveland Urban League (January 29, 1972); and a third to the United Neighborhood Houses Annual Conference (March 2, 1972).

The Cleveland address is presented in this volume. Speaking at the fifty-fourth anniversary luncheon of the Cleveland Urban League, Jordan had a favorable setting to present his message. In Cleveland the citizens had elected Carl Stokes the first black mayor of a major city, and had sent his brother Louis Stokes to Congress.

Jordan speaks enthusiastically about his country and perceptively about its problems. In his July speech he told the delegates:

> Black people today, for all our righteous anger and forceful dissent, still believe in the American dream. . . . We believe because this is our land, too. And we must, in this year of doubt and confusion, remind a forgetting nation that this land is ours. . . . This nation too often forgets that this land, this America, is sprinkled with our sweat, watered with our tears, and fertilized with our blood.

In Cleveland he extended this theme. By his carefully chosen language he is able to catch the yearnings of black America and to present his thoughts in the context of the nation's struggles and its failure to cope with long-smoldering racial problems. He puts his thought well when he says, "The central civil rights issue of the seventies . . . is the restucturing of America's economic and political power so that black people have their fair share of the rewards, the responsibilities, and the decision making in every sector of our common society."

[1] Address delivered at the annual meeting, Cleveland Urban League, January 28, 1972, Cleveland, Ohio. Quoted by permission.
[2] For biographical note, see Appendix.

Educated at DePauw University, a liberal arts college of distinction, Jordan, not many years ago, won first prize in the Indiana Interstate Oratorical Contest. Into his speeches he sprinkles well-chosen facts and examples (see the reference to his grandfather in this speech) and eloquent passages of poetry to give grace to what he says. His words are simple and appropriate; his sentences are direct and forceful. Jordan promises to be one of the better speakers of this period.

Last week the President of the United States, in his State of the Union address, very accurately described the mood of the nation. "We have been undergoing self-doubts, self-criticism," he said. "But these are only the other side of our growing sensitivity to the persistence of want in the midst of plenty, of our impatience with the slowness with which our age-old ills are being overcome."

The prevailing mood of self-doubt and self-criticism is without parallel in our times. We ask, "Are we a sick society?" The Gallup Poll reports that nearly half the people fear "a real breakdown in this country." The Roper organization finds that nearly two thirds of the American people believe the nation has lost its proper sense of direction. The country is in the throes of a deep-seated crisis of spirit, a crisis whose resolution calls for a harnessing of the moral energies of the society and for bold leadership that will carve a righteous path out of the wilderness of the soul.

The core of America's problems are racial. So long as black people suffer disproportionate disadvantage in almost every sphere of life, our society will be racked by guilt and agitation. So long as poor black people and poor white people are set against each other, scrambling for the crumbs from the table of an affluent society, this nation shall be troubled in mind and in spirit.

The time has come for America's dispossessed to come together, to formulate strategies that will unite and not divide, that will mobilize and not polarize. Black people, by forging solidarity and a spirit of pride, have inspired other Americans to rediscover their heritage and to treasure their ethnic backgrounds. It is my hope that black people, by forcefully exposing the inequities and the exploitation in our society, will similarly inspire other groups to focus their prime attentions on bringing about the changes that will benefit all Americans.

Cleveland is a microcosm for all America. It too suffers from the current economic depression. It too is polarized and torn by suspicion and dissent. It too stands at the brink of fiscal bankruptcy, a victim of the moral and social bankruptcy of a nation that spends billions on a jungle war or on space trips but cannot afford to insure full employment and schools and housing. Cleveland too has high barriers to black achievement. Its black citizens are confined to ghettos; its black workers are unemployed at a rate two and three times those for white workers, and many of its white citizens shrink from the kind of full and equal partnership with blacks that could help bring this city together again.

If change is to come, it will require the kind of bold leadership and human skills possessed by the city's business, labor and civic leaders. It will take above all a deep and abiding commitment to social change by the very people who have the power to bring about change. It will take an affirmation of belief in the principles of equality and concern with making this a truly open, democratic society. We in this nation will continue down the bitter path of racial strife and division until the men and women who hold responsible positions in this society—those who have made it—care about those who have not.

The Urban League is a vehicle for change, just as it remains a vehicle for those who must channel their energies and resources into building a better community. We have been and will continue to be:

> forceful advocates for the cause of black people and other minorities
> a result-oriented, issue-oriented organization dedicated to serving the people

a bridge between the races, forging unity and harmony
in a land torn by strife and friction
forthright believers in an open, pluralistic, integrated
society

The Urban League's task is a grave one, especially at this
time of growing despair that this nation can ever solve the
racial divisions that have so torn and bloodied the fabric
of our society. Much of white America's attitude seems
to be frozen in sullen resentment against what it interprets
as a capitulation to blacks in the sixties. Many middle Americans seem to be complaining that: "They've got their laws.
We've more clearly defined their rights. We've hired a few;
voted for one. A black doctor just moved into our suburban
neighborhood. We eat with them in restaurants; sit beside
them in buses; and even allowed a few to desegregate our
schools—on a token basis, of course. What more do they
want?"

But while black Americans are saying "a little bit of
freedom won't do," the apparent response is "thus far for
black folk—and no further." Hence, there appears to be a
national impasse founded on the reluctance of white Americans to complete the moral and social revolution started
in the sixties, and their widespread inability to fully understand that the issues of that decade are no longer the civil
rights issues of the seventies.

The civil rights issues of the sixties have changed. In the
sixties, the issue was the right to sit on the bus; today the
issue is where that bus is going and what does it cost to get
there. In the sixties, the issue was the right to eat at the lunch
counter; today the issue is the hunger and malnutrition that
stalk the land. In the sixties, the issue was fair employment
opportunity. Today, that can no longer be separated from
full employment of minority people and equal access to
every kind and level of employment up to and including
top policy-making jobs.

The central civil rights issue of the seventies then, is the restructuring of America's economic and political power so that black people have their fair share of the rewards, the responsibilities, and the decision making in every sector of our common society.

This demands a more sophisticated strategy than the marches and demonstrations of the past. We are no longer engaged in a moral struggle for the conscience of the nation, nor is the civil rights thrust still focused on the Old Confederacy. If we've learned anything about the new issues, it is that racism is not just a southern phenomenon, but that it is endemic to all America. And we have learned, too, that other sections of the country can react with as much violence, repression and irrationality today as the South has historically.

Black people in the seventies will no longer be comforted by the stirring resolve sung in the sixties: "ain't gonna let nobody turn us 'round," because when they see the new Supreme Court, they'll know we've been turned around. Black people will no longer find the same inspiration in the words of the black woman walking in the Montgomery bus boycott who said: "My feets is tired but my soul is rested." The fact today is that not only are her feet tired, but they hurt, and her soul is not rested, but tested, 'cause her spirit is broken and made low.

Marches on Washington won't pass a fair and equitable welfare reform bill, but blacks marching to the ballot box might. Irrational opposition to busing and lawsuits are no guarantee to stop the school buses, but integrated suburbs and neighborhoods and quality education for all might. Corporate responsibility won't amount to much if it's limited to signing up as equal opportunity employers, hiring a few black workers, and donating a bit less to the Urban League than to the company president's alma mater. But it might take on a new meaning if corporate executives left their offices and went into the ghetto to see for themselves what it is like to be poor and black in this America in 1972. And that goes too, for the Administration in Washington.

It must understand the human suffering and the human aspirations behind the walls of the rotting tenements and crumbling shacks. It must understand that the Federal resources made available to the Urban League must go hand in hand with a dramatic commitment to change, and with steady and relentless positive action on the broad range of issues affecting minority people.

Yes, this new civil rights era will be less dramatic and, perhaps at first, less popular. It will be an era of trench warfare, requiring, instead of charismatic leadership, knowledgeable technicians skillfully monitoring and exposing racism in the twilight zone of America's institutional policy-making processes. The battle has shifted from the streets to the deliberations of legislative committees, zoning boards and school boards. This new era is one of hard work, selfless sacrifice, and the sophisticated techniques of planning, analysis, and synthesis.

And the Urban League must embark upon new strategies fitting to this new era. One of the first programs we will undertake in the coming year will be to institute a new program of voter registration in the North and West to help bring about the "political browning of America" that we hope will be a giant step toward redressing the powerlessness of urban minorities. The great strides made by black southerners in recent years have been directly related to their growing use of the right to vote, and it is their example we hope to bring north.

Our concern goes beyond the mere placement of blacks in some local elected offices. Cleveland knows from first-hand experience that the election of a black mayor does not necessarily bring with it the kinds of state and Federal resources that will allow the mayor to create the jobs, housing and education his constituents so desperately need. If the cities are in trouble today, it is because of the flagrant neglect of the basic needs of the poor by a nation whose war on poverty has been shamefully ended by an inglorious cease-fire.

Our concern is with the involvement of black people in the democratic process; with the achievement by black people of the kind of political power that will ensure that office-holders of whatever race are sensitive to the issues and interests affecting the black community. This is the democratic way. This is the way all other groups in our society ensure that government is responsive to their needs. This is the way of nonviolent peaceful change in a society that cries out for constructive change and for the revitalization of the democratic process.

The systematic deprivation of black people from the seats of this society's power is all-embracing. Across the country, there are some 1,800 black elected officials, but that figure is impressive only if we ignore the fact that there are 522,000 such positions at all levels of government. That means that black people, who make up 12 percent of the population, hold only three tenths of 1 percent of the elected positions in America's many levels of government. Senator Brooke, the only black man in the Senate, represents a 1 percent black share of that body's 100 senators. The crusading black caucus in the House of Representatives comes to 3 percent of the 435 congressmen. And even these figures look good when we try to find blacks at the Cabinet and sub-Cabinet level, or at the helm of regional departments or regulatory agencies.

The system continues to be stacked against black ballot power. Some of our handful of black congressmen are in danger of losing their seats through reapportionment by conservative state legislatures. In many northern cities, minorities and poor people are virtually excluded from the political process through antiquated registration procedures.

So a major civil rights objective now must be to mount a major drive to get neighborhood registration teams, weekend and night registration office hours, community registrars, and a simplified system of permanent registration.

The drive for political empowerment must go hand-in-hand with the drive for economic empowerment. It's not enough to point with pride at black income figures creeping slowly, point by point, to levels still less than two thirds of white income. Economic empowerment means putting green dollars into black pockets and filling jobs at all levels with skilled black workers. Economic empowerment also means opening up the suburbs to blacks of all income levels so they can be near the new jobs that are coming on stream in suburban offices and plants. It means overcoming the irrational opposition heard from Forest Hills to Cleveland to scatter-site housing for the poor, so that they too can escape the imprisonment of slum housing and benefit from the schools and facilities of good neighborhoods.

And economic empowerment is what the Cleveland Urban League is bringing to thousands of minority citizens in this community, in the face of a job drain that has hit this city harder than many others. The Urban League has found jobs for eight hundred returning veterans. It was a driving force in the coalition that helped get the Cleveland Plan agreement and has already placed apprentices in five construction trade unions. Although it's only been in operation for fifteen months, the storefront Street Academy Program has enrolled 160 students. These are young people the public schools have pushed out and they bear the label of dropouts and failures. But of the first fifteen Street Academy graduates, fourteen are now in college. In the crucial field of housing, the Cleveland Urban League's Operation Equality has brought about agreements with the managers of some 15,000 houses and apartments that will open these units up to black renters and black building workmen.

Impressive as this record is, it is but a mere indication of the kinds of things the Urban League could do if it were adequately funded and staffed. The truth of the matter is that the problems facing black people in Cleveland are so deep and so profound, that the League is literally inundated by cries for help, some of which must, of necessity, go unanswered. Every single day of the week about one hundred people come to the Urban League's office seeking jobs, housing, help with local bureaucracies, help for the teenager on drugs, help for the crushing burdens that press down upon anyone who is poor and black in this America of ours.

The Urban League deals on a daily basis with America's failure to respond to the needs of its black and poor citizens. It has helped thousands to win better jobs, housing, and education, and it has been the catalyst for community coalitions and joint efforts to make this a better, healthier city. If it has done so much with so little, how much more it could do if it had the resources and the increased support of the responsible, concerned leaders of this region.

The Urban League movement must continue to be effective. We must deliver. We cannot fail.

For if the Urban League fails in its mission, America fails in its purpose. But the Urban League cannot fail for another reason—there is a constituency out there depending on us. There are black folk out there who never heard our name and don't understand what we do who are depending on us.

Depending on us are those black people who have no hope or hope of hope.

Depending on us are those black people who cry out today, not for freedom and equality, but for a crust of bread and a morsel of meat.

Depending on us are little black children who cry out not for Black Power but for medicine for their festering sores and for protection from the rats and the roaches.

Depending on us is the junkie in the ghetto.

Depending on us is the unemployed father, the underemployed daughter, the welfare-dependent mother, and the son home from Vietnam who can't find work.

Depending on us are black folk like Grandpa Jim Griggs who, when he was seventy years old sat talking with me on the porch of his broken-down roadside shanty in southwest Georgia, where he spent his life as a sharecropper. "Pa," I asked, "What is it that you want most out of life at seventy?" And Pa said, "Junior, I just want to go to the bathroom indoors in a warm place one time before I die."

Depending on us are black people just like Pa who can't deal with the issues that galvanize those more fortunate than they—issues like integration or separation, pan-Africanism and nation-building, voting Republican or Democrat. The issues for these black folk boil down to one big issue— SURVIVAL!

It is for these black Americans that the Urban League exists. It is to their cause that the Urban League is dedicated. It is their agenda and their needs that must shape our policies. And it is their interests we must advance as we seek to forge a future that is more just and humane.

Like the tree planted by the rivers of water, we shall not be moved from our sacred mission to make this a land of freedom, justice and complete equality.

SEEKING A LINK WITH THE PAST [3]

PATSY T. MINK [4]

"America is not a country which needs to punish its dissenters to preserve its honor. . . . America is not a country which needs to demand conformity of all its people, for its strength lies in all our diversities converging in one common belief, that of the importance of freedom as the essence of our country." In this passage from a speech made in the House of Representatives, Mrs. Patsy T. Mink, Representative-at-large from Hawaii, expressed an important part of her philosophy. She has been called "the most prominent woman in Hawaiian politics since Queen Liliuokalani." During her service in Washington since 1966 she has stood for liberal legislation promoting education, equal employment opportunities, equal rights for women, civil rights, aid to the elderly, student financial aid, better treatment of the territories, and the ending of the war in Vietnam.

She was an ideal choice to speak to the 30th Anniversary and Installation Banquet of the West Los Angeles Japanese-American Citizens League on November 6, 1971. In attendance were 350 persons, not only Japanese-Americans but members of other ethnic groups as well. Of Japanese descent, Mrs. Mink knows well the prejudice against Asians. With memories of her own youth, and as the mother of a college-age daughter who attends the University of Chicago, Mrs. Mink can speak with authority about the problems of youth adjustment and for understanding of the Third World movement. She has said of herself, "What I bring to Congress is an Hawaiian background of tolerance and equality that can contribute a great deal to better understanding between races."

Mrs. Mink is pure Japanese and a third-generation Islander. In high school and college she participated in oratorical contests. In 1947 she won first place in the All Hawaii Oratorical contest at the University of Hawaii. Dr. Elizabeth Carr, Professor Emeritus of Speech at the University of Hawaii, says that Mrs. Mink has "a warm, appealing voice," "a direct manner," and "a winning modesty." In 1968 the Pacific Speech Association gave her its annual award as the Community Speaker of the Year in recognition of her effectiveness as a speaker.

[3] Address was delivered before the West Los Angeles Japanese-American Citizens League, Airport Marina Hotel, Playa Del Rey, California, November 6, 1971. Quoted by permission.

[4] For biographical note, see Appendix.

I would like to thank President Kanegai and the other officers and members of the West Los Angeles Japanese-American Citizens League for this opportunity to be with you at your thirtieth anniversary banquet and installation. I am delighted to participate in this memorable occasion.

It must be difficult to look back thirty years to 1941 and relive the pains and agonies that were inflicted upon you as citizens, unloved and unwanted in their own country of their birth. Loving this land as much as any other citizen, it is difficult to fathom the despair and fury which many must have felt, yet who fought back and within a few years had reestablished their lives and their futures. Most of us remember these years vividly. Our faith in justice was tested many times over. Our patriotism was proven by blood of our sons upon the battlefields.

Yet today, thirty years later to many even in this room, it is only a part of our history. Our children, thirty years old and younger, cannot follow with us these memories of the forties. They tire of our stories of the past. Their life is now, today . . . tomorrow. Their youthful fervor was poured into the symbolism of the repeal of Title II of the Internal Security Act of 1950, portrayed by its title, Emergency Detention Act. That Act became law nearly ten years *after* the Japanese were evacuated from the West Coast into "relocation camps." Yet, it stood as a reminder of what could happen again. Of course, despite the successful repeal, it could happen again, as it did indeed to the Japanese-Americans who were rounded up without any statutory authority whatsoever. It was not until 1950 that Title II became law.

It is quite evident that I am standing before an affluent group whose surface appearance does not reveal the years of struggle and doubt that have ridden behind you.

Sociologists have generally described the Japanese-Americans as an easily acculturated people who quickly assimilated the ways of their surroundings. This has always been in my view a friendly sort of jab at our cultural background, for what it has come to mean for me is a description of a conformist which I hope I am not!

I still dream that I shall be able to be a real participant in the changing scenario of opportunity for all of America. In this respect, I share the deep frustration and anguish of our youth as I see so much around us that cries out for our attention and that we continue to neglect.

Many factors have contributed towards a deepening sense of frustration about our inability to solve our problems of poverty and racial prejudice. Undoubtedly the prolonged, unending involvement in Vietnam has contributed to this sense of hopelessness. At least for our youth who must bear the ultimate burden of this war, it seems unfair that they should be asked to serve their country in this way when there are so many more important ways in which their youth and energy can be directed to meet the urgent needs at home. They view our Government as impotent to deal with these basic issues.

It is true that Congress has passed a great many civil rights laws. The fact that new, extra laws were found necessary to make it easier for some people to realize their constitutional guarantees is a sad enough commentary on the American society, but what is even worse is the fact that the majority of our people are still unready, personally, to extend these guarantees to all despite the Constitution and all the civil rights laws, and despite their protestations to the contrary.

Certainly, no one will admit his bigotry and prejudice —yet we always find ways to clothe such feelings in more presentable forms—and few will openly advocate suppression or oppression of other men, but nevertheless, it exists.

Although Congress has repealed the Emergency Detention Act, the fight for freedom is not over. We now see a new witch hunt proclaimed in which all Government employees will be examined for their memberships and organizations. It seems that we have not yet succeeded in expunging the notion that "dangerous" persons can be identified by class or group relationships and punished accordingly.

I believe that nobody can find safety in numbers—by huddling with the larger mass in hopes of being overlooked. Those who seek to suppress will always find ways to single out others. Instead, we must change the basic attitude that all must conform or be classed as renegades and radicals. Our nation was founded on the idealistic belief in individualism and pioneering spirit, and it would be tragic for our own generation to forswear that ideal for the false security of instant assimilation.

It seems to me that our society is large enough to accept a wide diversity of types and opinions, and that no group should be forced to try to conform to the image of the population as a whole. I sometimes wonder if our goal as Japanese-Americans is to be so like the White Anglo-Saxon Protestant population as to be indistinguishable from it. If so, we will obviously never succeed!

There has been and continues to be prejudice in this country against Asians. The basis of this is the belief that the Oriental is "inscrutable." Having such base feelings, it is simple to stir up public outrage against the recognition of the People's Republic of China in the United Nations, for instance, even though reasoned judgment dictates otherwise, unless of course a Yellow Communist is really worse than a Red one!

The World War II detention overnight reduced the entire population of one national origin to an enemy, stripped of property, rights of citizenship, human dignity, and due process of law, without so much as even a stifled voice of conscience among our leading scholars or civil libertarians. More recently, the Vietnam war has reinforced the view of Orientals as something less than fully human. All Vietnamese stooping in the rice fields are pictured as the enemy, subhuman without emotions and for whom life is less valuable than for us.

During the trial of Lieutenant Calley, we were told about "MGR," the "Mere Gook Rule" which was the underlying basis for Calley's mindless assertion that the slaughter of defenseless women and children, our prisoners of war, was "no big thing." The "Mere Gook Rule" holds that life is less important, less valuable to an Oriental.

Laws that protect other human beings do not apply to "gooks." One reporter noted before the verdict became known that the essence of the Calley case was to determine the validity of this rule. He described it as the "unspoken issue" at the trial.

The issue was not as unspoken as most would prefer to believe. The indictment drawn up by the Army against Lieutenant Calley stated in six separate charges that he did at My Lai murder four "Oriental human beings" . . . murder not less than thirty "Oriental human beings" . . . murder three "Oriental human beings" . . . murder an unknown number of "Oriental human beings" not less than seventy . . . and so on numbering 102. Thus, the Army did not charge him with the murder of human beings as presumably would have been the case had Caucasians been involved, but instead charged the apparently lesser offense of killing mere "Oriental human beings."

The Army's definition of the crime is hardly surprising inasmuch as the Army itself could have been construed as on trial along with Calley for directing a genocide against the Vietnamese. Indeed, the Lieutenant pleaded he was only doing what he thought the Army wanted. It seems clear to me that the Army recognized the "Mere Gook Rule" officially by distinguishing between the murder of human beings and "Oriental human beings." When Calley was convicted, the resulting thunder of criticism verified that many in the public also went along with the concept of differing scales of humanity.

Somehow, we must put into perspective Dean Rusk's dread of the "yellow peril" expressed as justification for a massive antiballistics missile system on the one hand, and on the other, a quest for improved relations with Peking. This latter event could have a great meaning in our own lives as Japanese-Americans. We could help this country begin to deal with Asians as people. Just the other day in a beauty parlor, I heard a congressional secretary discuss China and say, "An Asian is different, you can never figure out what he's really thinking. He has so little value for life!"

Instead of seeking refuge, we should seek to identify as Asians, and begin to serve America as the means by which she can come to understand the problems of the East. Our talents have not been used in American diplomacy, I suspect, largely because we are still not trusted enough.

We must teach our country that life is no less valuable, and human dignity no less precious, in Asia than elsewhere. Our detractors point to the large-scale killings that have occurred in China, Vietnam, Pakistan, and elsewhere in Asia, but we hear remarkably few references to the mass-slaughter of six million Jews in Nazi gas chambers in World War II—that was done by Aryans, not Asians, and the total far exceeds the loss of life in the Orient that has been used to justify the debasement of "mere gooks." I am not trying to compare one group against another, but merely to point out that a lack of appreciation for the value of human life can occur wherever totalitarian government exists. This makes it more than vital for us to oppose such influences within our own country wherever they may occur. The war in Vietnam has lasted for seven years. If Americans believed there was the same worth in the life of an Asian, this war would have ended long ago. If Americans were willing to concede that the Asian mind was no different than his, a peace would have been forged in Paris long ago. I am convinced that racism is at the heart of this immoral policy.

I know that many of you are puzzled and even dismayed by actions of some of your sons and daughters who have insisted on a more aggressive role in combating the war and other evils that exist in our society. I plead with you for understanding of this Third World movement in which not only young Japanese-Americans but many minority groups are so deeply involved.

We are confronted with what seem to be many different revolutions taking place all over the world . . . the black revolution, the revolution of emerging nations, the youth revolution here and in other countries as well—and something that was even more unheard of, the priests challenging the Vatican on the most basic issues of celibacy and birth control. It is no accident that these things are all happening at the same time, for they all stem from the same great idea that has somehow been rekindled in the world, and that is the idea that the individual is important.

All of the systems of the world today have this in common: for they are mainly concerned with industrialization, efficiency, and gross national product; the value of Man is forgotten.

The children of some of you here tonight are involved in the great protests of today—are they chronic malcontents and subversives? I think not—I think they are probably fairly well-educated, thoughtful people who see certain conditions they don't like and are trying to do something about it. I'm not sure they know exactly what they want to do. I do know they are clearly dissatisfied with the way their world has been run in the past.

So, the problem is not what to do about dissent among our young people—the problem is what to do about the causes of this dissent. The question is not "how to suppress the dissent" but how to make it meaningful . . . how to make it productive of a better society which truly places high value on individual human beings *as* human beings and not merely as so many cogs in the great, cold and impersonal machinery of an industrialized society.

I, for one, believe that the grievances of our youth are real and that they are important. Merely because the majority of students are not involved . . . merely because the dissidents are few . . . should not minimize the need for serious efforts to effectuate change. Our eighteen-year-olds now have the right to vote. Whether we like it or not, we will have to take better account of their wishes. Their acceptance as adults will bring into policy making eleven million new voters next year. Their cause for identity must be encouraged.

Our sons and daughters seek to establish a link with the past. They want to discover who they are, why they are here, and where their destinies are to take them. So many of our children are growing up in complete isolation in a society that places a premium on conformity, in middle-class homes where parents still want to play down their differences, and prefer to homogenize with society. Some of these children are rebelling and are seeking ways to preserve their uniqueness and their special heritage. I see pride and strength in this.

One of the most promising avenues for this renewed search for one's heritage is in our school systems—the logical place for instructing children in the knowledge they need. Programs of Ethnic Heritage Studies are needed in our schools. I feel that this would be particularly valuable in Hawaii, California and other areas where there are large numbers of children of Oriental descent.

It seems to me that we as Asians have a large stake in encouraging and promoting such a program. We cannot and must not presume knowledge about Asia merely because we are Asians. This requires concentrated study and dedicated determination. Of course, we do not need to become scholars cloistered in the ivory tower of some campus. We need to become aware of the enormous history of Asia and through our daily lives, regardless of what our profession, translate it to all the people with whom we deal. We have not fully met our responsibility to educate the public about Asia and its people.

I hope that all Japanese-American organizations and others with strong beliefs in the magnificent history and culture of the Orient will now help lead the way to a more enlightened America. We have an immense story to tell, for as I have said the public at large too often assumes that all civilization is Western and no worth is given to the human values of the East. As long as this belief persists, we will have future Vietnams. The way to counteract it is to build public knowledge, through school courses, travel, and dedicated emphasis on increased communications, so that our people will know and appreciate all that is Asian.

Last Thursday night in a display of utter ignorance and contempt for diversity, the House of Representatives killed the ethnic heritage studies program by a vote of 200 ayes to 159 noes. And so you see, I speak of an urgent matter. We are so few and they who do not care to understand us are so numerous.

It is fine for all citizens to pursue the good life and worldly goods on which our society places such emphasis, but there is increasing recognition that all will be ashes in our mouths unless our place as individuals is preserved. This is what the young are seeking—and I am among those who would rejoice in their goals.

They need the guidance and support of their parents to succeed, but in any event with or without us, they are trying. It behooves us to do all we can to accept their aspirations, if not all of their actions, in the hope that this new generation will be able to find a special role for themselves in America, to help build her character, to define her morality, to give her a depth in soul, and to make her realize the beauty of our diverse society with many races and cultures of which we are one small minority.

LA RAZA AND THE LAW [5]

Edward M. Kennedy [6]

Like other minorities the Mexican-Americans, or Chicanos as they prefer to be called, are bitter over the injustices that they have encountered throughout the Southwest. They know discrimination and prejudice almost as devastating as that which blacks have lived with in the South. David F. Gomez, a Mexican-American writer, says, "Prejudice, that occasionally surfaces on a large scale, continues on a day-to-day basis in the barrio. Verbal abuse and physical harassment are a way of life" (*America,* June 26, 1971). Signs of tension were the riots in East Los Angeles in September 1970 and the tragic death of popular newsman Ruben Salazar. Desperation has spawned violence.

Much of the discontent among Chicanos centers around alleged police brutality and harassment, prejudiced district attorneys and judges, and the seeming inability of Mexican-Americans to get what they think is a fair trial. At present there are about 600 Chicano lawyers to serve a Mexican-American population of 10 million. In Texas and California only 1.5 percent of all attorneys are Chicanos.

The Kennedy image, particularly that of Robert, remains strong in the minds of many Mexican-Americans. For example, Albert Pena, Jr., in an address to the Council on Community Action, Bexar County, Texas, said:

> Robert Kennedy repudiated the middle of the road and people responded all over this nation. For he had not only the charm, grace and wit of all the Kennedys, but he also had the commitment and the courage we needed in a leader. (*Congressional Record,* March 3, 1972, page S 3239)

This statement is particularly interesting in light of Edward M. Kennedy's reference to his brother when he says: "Robert Kennedy . . . walked through the barrios of East Los Angeles and through the dusty fields of Delano. He was committed to change the conditions of poverty and discrimination he saw." As many have pointed out, Edward M. Kennedy lives in the afterglow of his two martyred brothers. Many of the poor and unfortunate

---

[5] Address delivered to the Conference on the Spanish-Speaking and the Law, Georgetown University Law School, Washington, D.C., March 3, 1972.

[6] For biographical note, see Appendix.

turn to him for leadership in their struggles to be heard. This fact probably explains why he was invited to speak on March 3, 1972, to the Conference on the Spanish-Speaking and the Law at Georgetown University Law School, Washington, D. C. The meeting was sponsored by the Georgetown Chapter of La Raza National Law Students Association. La Raza is a nation-wide organization of Mexican-Americans formed in 1968 to coordinate their efforts to achieve civil rights and equal opportunities.

I am pleased to be able to meet with you this morning and to open this conference on La Raza and the law.

At the outset, let me express my pleasure and support for the decision of the Georgetown chapter of La Raza National Law Student Association to undertake this venture.

Without the full and forceful advocacy of change, without the public demand for an end to the inequities of the past, and without the commitment of the young leaders of the Spanish-speaking community, nothing will ever be accomplished.

It has been my view for many years that the Chicano and Puerto Rican communities not only needed to press demands on the institutions of government, but on the political parties as well. For too long, we have all been slow to recognize the needs of the Spanish-speaking community.

Perhaps the most depressing fact to recognize is how long the evil of discrimination has been permitted to continue.

Octavio Paz, perhaps one of the Western Hemisphere's most eloquent essayists, wrote in 1950 of the Chicanos he had met in Los Angeles: "They have lived in the city for many years," he said, "wearing the same clothes and speaking the same language as the other inhabitants . . . yet no one would mistake them for authentic North Americans . . . they are instinctive rebels and North American racism has vented its wrath on them more than once."

In California, and the states of the Southwest, the failure to promote equality of opportunity is impossible to understand and impossible to deny.

It seems difficult, when one looks at the evidence of discrimination, to recall that the California constitution was penned in both English and Spanish. It seems difficult to remember that one third of its signers were Spanish-surnamed Californians.

Yet the equal rights and privileges guaranteed to the Chicanos by state and Federal constitutions have been denied not once but time and time again. And it is no wonder that young Chicanos have exploded in anger.

Their outrage is documented in the files of the United States Civil Rights Commission, in the hearing record of the Senate Select Committee on Equal Education, in the complaint file of the Equal Employment Opportunity Commission.

But most tragically, their outrage is documented in the lives and deaths of Ruben Salazar, Romulo Avalos, and others, men who should not have died when they did, or how they did.

And these deaths are irrevocably bound in the oppressive conditions faced by far too many of the Spanish-speaking citizens of this land, conditions which make a sham and shuck of our professed allegiance to equality and justice for all.

Fewer than two out of three Mexican-American students in California alone complete high school. In the Southwest, the figures are worse, barely half of those who begin complete the twelfth grade. Among Puerto Ricans, in my own city of Boston, the figures are at least as bad. With 7,800 school-age children, there are reports of less than half enrolled and the number of high school graduates in recent years has rarely even totaled ten.

Ethnic isolation of Spanish-speaking students shows the dismal effect of educational gerrymandering with two thirds of the students attending ethnically imbalanced schools.

In the Southwest, barely 4 percent of the teachers are Mexican-American and only 3 percent of the principals, yet nearly 20 percent of the students are Chicanos.

In the states of Colorado, New Mexico and Texas, Anglo high-school graduates are twice as likely to enter college as Mexican-Americans.

But I know those statistics merely tell half the story.

They do not tell the anguish of the school child who is told it is wrong to speak Spanish. Nor the frustration of being told that the college prep program is closed. Nor the most grievous wrong, that of assigning an unknown number of Spanish-speaking children to classes for mentally retarded because of their scores on English language tests they could not understand. Equal education has been denied to the Spanish-speaking and it is time to change.

In employment, the statistics are equally disheartening. In the nation as a whole the average income of the Chicano adult is more than $2,000 a year less than the average income of Anglos.

Less than 4 percent of the state jobs in California were held by Mexican-Americans a year ago despite the fact that they represent 16 percent of the state's population.

And in New York City, a Puerto Rican man is three times as likely to be unemployed as whites. Equal employment has been denied to the Spanish-speaking and it is time to change.

Equality before the law is a concept ingrained in the American heritage. Yet for Chicanos, it remains a far-off goal.

The Civil Rights Commission found a "widespread pattern of police misconduct against Mexican-Americans in the Southwest."

The California Rural Legal Assistance Project documented the exclusion of Mexican-Americans from grand jury lists. They found a twelve-year period in which 500,000 Spanish-surnamed persons were eligible for grand jury duty in Los Angeles County, yet only four were chosen.

Perhaps the most disturbing incidents are those that still occur at the Federal level. Why was it necessary for senators to send telegrams to spur the Justice department to investigate an assassination plot against Cesar Chavez?

And why was it necessary for senators to remind the Labor department that their own regulations prohibited importing foreign workers to break a farmworker strike?

And if we look at the Selective Service System, once again, we find inequities. Practically no change has occurred in the representation of the Spanish-speaking community on local and appeal boards. On local boards it was 2.9 percent in 1968, and today it is barely 4 percent. On appeal boards, it is even worse, barely over 3 percent. And when one looks at the states with heavy concentrations of Spanish-speaking, one finds only 4 of 88 appeal board members in California who are Spanish-speaking. In Colorado, none. In Arizona, none. In Florida, none. Yet these are the boards that the system provides to halt the egregious errors that many local boards commit. How can that cleansing function be fulfilled when none of the appeal boards can easily understand, let alone relate to, a Spanish-speaking registrant?

Equal treatment under the law, a basic condition for maintaining the bond of citizenship, has been repeatedly and flagrantly denied to the Spanish-speaking and it is time to change.

These statistics demonstrate the need for the seminar that is taking place today. More than that, they demonstrate the absolute necessity for Spanish-speaking citizens to be active politically. For if you permit the political leadership of this country to continue to treat you as "strangers in your own land," then there will be a perennial list of unmet goals in education, housing, in employment, in access to the protection of the law.

The challenge not only lies with both parties to respond and to respond effectively. It lies also with you to force the parties to respond. And despite the tremendous resistance that undoubtedly exists, I believe that they can be made to respond.

But it means that you must take the initiative, that you must do the registering and organizing, that you must do the precinct work and the polling. And it is not just the Federal elections that count. Governors choose boards of regents and state university directors. Sheriffs and district attorneys decide local law enforcement policies and city councilmen and mayors control the decisions that send funds to the manicured streets of the affluent few or the still-unpaved roads of the barrio.

The challenge is before you. It does not rest with those unwilling to risk something of themselves. Nor does it rest with those who demand that the struggle be easily won. It rests only with those ready to trade the comfort and convenience of the critic for the torment and sacrifice of the committed.

Yet you have among La Raza many who already have shown the way. You have men such as Cesar Chavez, who has brought the farmworker of this nation his first hope for lasting dignity. The victory in Florida is part of a struggle that began not five or ten years ago, but two decades ago when the first organizing began.

And if that kind of commitment is made, then I believe there will be response. I believe there must be response.

Robert Kennedy shared that view. He walked through the barrios of East Los Angeles and through the dusty fields of Delano. He was committed to change the conditions of poverty and discrimination he saw.

For he believed as I do, that this nation can never be free until there is no longer a child who cries from hunger or a mother who fears illness because she cannot afford a doctor, or a man who dies because the law does not see him as a man.

There is much to be done before we are free.

INAUGURAL ADDRESS
OF THE CHIEF OF THE CHEROKEES [7]

W. W. KEELER [8]

The speech reprinted below was delivered in a remote part of Oklahoma. It is a speech full of meaning and sentiment, for it expresses the heartfelt wishes, the suffering and striving of the Cherokees, who refuse to surrender their identity and who wish to steer their own course and determine their own fate.

In this inaugural address W. W. Keeler puts into words the heroic theme of this courageous people. Attuned to their story, he reminds them, "This is a historic moment for all Cherokees, Delawares, and Shawnees. It marks the return of the management of their tribal affairs into the hands of the people." He is referring to the fact that he is the first *elected* chief in sixty-four years. After 1907, when Oklahoma was granted statehood, the President of the United States appointed the chiefs.

The Cherokee story supports Keeler's characterization of his tribe as "a dauntless people." In May 1838, Federal troops rounded up tribe members who had refused to leave their native North Carolina and drove them over a "Trail of Tears," so called because of the hunger, disease, suffering, and death which attended the march. In spite of hardships, dissension, persecution, and destitution, the Cherokees persisted as a people through the years. They made Tahlequah, Oklahoma, located in the green hills of the northeastern part of the state, their national capital and the center for tribal functions.

W. W. Keeler, chairman and chief executive officer of the Phillips Petroleum Company and the 1970 chairman of the National Association of Manufacturers, is a recognized speaker who has addressed such organizations as the Economic Club of Detroit (April 20, 1970) and the Executive Club of Chicago (January 22, 1971). A close observer of his speaking has characterized his delivery as "direct" and his manner as "sincere and warm." On this particular day he spoke with considerable emotion.

[7] Address delivered September 4, 1971, Tahlequah, Oklahoma. Quoted by permission.

[8] For biographical note, see Appendix.

Deputy Commissioner Crowe, Chaplain Ketcher, Senator McSpadden and chiefs of the Indian tribes of Oklahoma who honor us by their presence here today, fellow Cherokees, friends, ladies and gentlemen.

This is a historic moment for all Cherokees, Delawares, and Shawnees. It marks the return of the management of their tribal affairs into the hands of the people. We have not had this responsibility of self-determination for more than threescore years. I am proud and happy to see this day. I am honored to be your elected leader.

The Cherokees were a free and independent nation, with a constitutional government elected by the people, almost a century and a half ago.

In the years between then and now, our forebears and we suffered internal strife, removal to an alien land, a civil war that was not of our making, loss of our land without fair compensation, discrimination because of our color, and indignity because we were few in number.

Our Delaware and Shawnee brothers joined us by purchase agreement to share in our hopes and sorrows and in the lean production of the rocky hillsides to which the Cherokees had been driven.

But we are a dauntless people. Our fathers would not bow to a stronger force. Neither have we ever bowed to it. Not when we were penniless; nor when we were without food to fill our children's stomachs.

Not when we were without clothing to shield us against bitter winds that howl in the forgotten hollows between these hills; nor when these hallowed grounds on which we stand were a place of mockery and contempt for those who had herded us onto them.

We were dauntless in our defeat. We remembered the hardships of those who gave us our heritage. We took courage from their example. We would not be overcome. The blood of our fathers beats strongly in our veins; and we can still hear the distant drums that echo against the mountainsides of the lost and lonely memories that whisper along the byways of our hallowed heritage.

Today we see the beginning of the realization of everything that was only a dream during the lifetime of most of us here today.

The Cherokee nation was never dead; only asleep. Today it stirs and begins to awaken. Today our children see the dream that you and I have had for so many bleak years.

We are again entrusted with the management of our own affairs. We are now free to elect our own leaders. We are free to train our people for jobs; to improve the educational opportunities of our children; to provide adequate medical care for all who need it; to record and promote our noble heritage.

We must be united if we are to accomplish the heavy work that lies ahead. We must join hands with all of our brothers as never before in the history of our people.

Past mistakes and animosity must be laid aside. All of us have been mistaken at some time in the past. We must learn from those mistakes. If we fail in this, the opportunity of this moment will be lost—perhaps beyond recall.

We must think of the work to be done in the future; not of what we should have done in the past.

My opponents in the election came forward with many good proposals. I intend to ask their help and support in making them part of the goals of my administration for the coming four years. I ask everyone to join with me in bringing about their benefits for the Cherokees and their brothers, the Delawares and the Shawnees.

We must develop the human resources of our people. We must end any inequities of tribal activities that may have developed in the past years. All of our programs must be fair to all of our people. The tribal rolls must be brought up to date to include our children as well as our fathers. We must standardize the Cherokee language. I agree that the chief or vice chief should speak Cherokee.

I recognize that our Cherokee executive committee, of which I have been a member, has been criticized. But I also know that they have given great service to the Cherokees. I want to express my thanks to them for their unselfish assistance to me. Certainly they should be continued until we have had time to rewrite our Cherokee constitution and make it possible for tribal leaders to be more responsive to individual Cherokees. I would like to see an executive and a legislative branch based on the pattern of our early-day constitution. The tribal government must reflect the will of all of the people.

I pledge to you today, in this historic setting, my time and the best of whatever talents I have.

I thank you for your support in years past; and for your confidence in me to lead the tribe for the next four years.

I humbly and sincerely ask for your support and for your best advice in the years ahead.

Together, we can accomplish even greater things than have been accomplished in the past. With God's help, we can bring about miracles even greater than the accomplishment of this day.

Cherokees! Give me your trust and your united support. Thank you.

CONSUMER INTERESTS

MEET THE PRESS [1]

RALPH NADER [2]

In six years Naderism has become an influential force on the American scene. As the champion of the consumer, Ralph Nader, son of Lebanese immigrants and a graduate of the Harvard Law School, has stirred significant interest in many consumer problems. "No other man in the country," says Michael T. Mallory "is so feared, loved, hated and yet so mysterious. . . . Ralph Nader is a prophet of a secular religion. . . . His gospel is individual responsibility. He calls it citizenship; others might call it ethics. Whatever you call it, the same theme runs through his shotgun blasts at government and industry and his innumerable speeches to advertising men, lawyers, engineers, and students" (*National Observer*, December 25, 1971). Elizabeth Drew suggests that he is "one of the most significant figures of this period" (New York *Times*, March 19, 1972).

Whether before a congressional committee, reporters, or a university audience, he commands attention and interest. He is reported to receive up to $3,000 for an appearance for lectures and to earn as much as $100,000 per year through his writing and speaking. From this income he supports his consumer organizations, of which there are four; at least a half dozen other crusading groups have spun off from the Nader movement and operate independently.

The great interest across the country in Nader made him an ideal guest for "Meet the Press: America's Press Conference of the Air," the weekly television and radio interview program aired by the National Broadcasting System. The program was telecast May 30, 1971, with Bill Monroe, NBC newscaster, serving as host. Nader faced queries from James J. Kilpatrick of the Washington Star Syndicate; James Bishop, Jr., of *Newsweek*; Lucia Mouat of *The Christian Science Monitor;* and Peter Hackes of NBC News.

[1] Television broadcast, 1:00-1:30 p.m., EDT, radio broadcast, 6:30-7:00 p.m., EDT, May 30, 1971, NBC Studios in Washington, D.C. Permission to publish granted by Lawrence E. Spivak, producer.

[2] For biographical note, see Appendix.

Nader's effectiveness probably comes not from his power as a speaker but from his sincerity and the urgency of his material. Before a live audience he speaks extemporaneously, stringing together one example after another and inserting interesting side remarks. He enlivens his development with well-placed bits of satirical humor. He crouches or sprawls over the lectern, resting on his left elbow while he gestures with his right arm. He looks back and forth from the lectern to his listeners, leaning forward when he becomes excited or eager to emphasize a point. He wears his black hair short, and his dress is neat and conservative. At a recent appearance at Louisiana State University he held a large audience rapt for well over an hour and then remained an additional hour and a half to answer questions. He has great rapport with college students.

Mr. Monroe: Our guest today on "Meet the Press" is the nation's leading crusader for consumer interests, Ralph Nader.

Mr. Hackes: Mr. Nader, for the last six or seven years now you have been conducting your consumer crusades. You have gone from automobiles to the environment, you have lashed out at regulatory agencies, you are into a study of the National Academy of Sciences, campaigning for cheaper airline fares, even a push for no smoking in buses. Some of your critics say that you probably have spaced yourself out just a little bit on the thin side.

What is your own personal appraisal of what you have accomplished?

Mr. Nader: As against the enormous number of problems, I think we are touching on a very small number of them, because our criteria is one of accuracy and one of the potential contributions which we can make. Those are the boundaries that decide what areas we go into. I think in terms of contributions there is an enormous amount of disclosure, getting the facts to the people, that we try to do, trying to give people an opportunity to have an impact on these problems, either through representatives or directly.

Mr. Hackes: But now you are even going international. Canada, Japan, Brazil. There are those who say that you could be immensely more influential if you narrowed your-self down and zeroed in on two or three important items.

MR. NADER: First, the so-called international activities are very peripheral to the impact of US companies in these countries, particularly in Quebec in the pollution of Union Carbide, but it is our impression, based on our experience and our soundings from citizens around the country that it is important for people to understand things are very much interrelated and that some people see a relationship to auto safety and some to nutrition in food and some to pollution and some to occupational safety. Not all people can be in-terested in all things. It is important to show people that the malaise of the country and the lack of accountability of large power centers in Government and business manifest them-selves not just in inadequate bumpers or high insurance pre-miums, but across the board. That is why we try to go into a number of very important areas and show these inter-relations.

MR. HACKES: You say there is a lot to be done. Just this month Maurice Stans, the Commerce Secretary, said that "Consumers receive full satisfaction from nearly every pur-chase they make from American business." If Mr. Stans is correct, or even largely correct, aren't you really wasting your time and effort on something that perhaps the people don't want or need?

MR. NADER: Obviously I don't think Mr. Stans is correct. He represents the business constituency in the Federal Gov-ernment and makes no bones about it. I would refer the public to documented studies, instead of wave-of-the-hand commentaries, done by the Senate Antitrust Committee and done by the Senate Commerce Committee, done by the Federal Trade Commission, and many other documentations showing there is too much price-fixing in the country, there is too much anticompetitive practice, there is too much shoddy merchandise, services in the automotive and other industries that are woefully inadequate. The nutritional level in foods is not what it should be. There is too much decep-

tive advertising. These are contentions that not only are
documented by consumer advocates, but they are beginning
to be shared by an increasing number of responsible businessmen in the community.

Mr. Kilpatrick: Mr. Nader, in an article in the May
issue of *Fortune* magazine, this was said of you: "The passion
that rules in him, and he is a passionate man, is aimed at
smashing utterly the target of his hatred, which is corporate
power."

How do you respond to that assessment?

Mr. Nader: That is a paranoid description by Mr. Armstrong who wrote the article. Of course, I thoroughly disagree with it and think it is utterly inaccurate. My interest
is in disciplining, along with other people who do this kind
of work, corporate power, and disciplining corporate power
—making it reach its potential—is a far cry from smashing it.
As a matter of fact, the entire economy in this country depends on responsible corporate power.

Mr. Kilpatrick: If you have left that impression with
Mr. Armstrong as a responsible writer, do you suppose you
might have left it with others also?

Mr. Nader: That is the first such article that has stated it
in that way.

Mr. Kilpatrick: He also said in this article that your
habit of coating your facts with invective and assigning the
worst possible motives to almost everyone but yourself has
made reform more difficult. Do you disagree with this appraisal also?

Mr. Nader: I am still looking for some examples.

Mr. Kilpatrick: What about the other day when you
were before the Senate Committee and you charged the auto
manufacturers with what you described as "criminal fraud."
Would that not seem to you invective?

Mr. Nader: No, that is not invective, that is a description
of a stated fact. Just like if somebody is engaged in burglar-
izing a building in a New York City street, it is called burglary, which is a crime.

MR. KILPATRICK: Could you identify even one corporation that in your judgment has done a good job, a responsible job in safety or in pollution?

MR. NADER: There are some corporations that are trying to make that effort, but not in the pollution area.

MR. KILPATRICK: None at all in pollution?

MR. NADER: No. They all respond to the same syndromes. That is, if a company is not going to be subjected to greater costs for polluting than not polluting, its internal economical calculus is to continue polluting because it doesn't have to pay the cost. The public pays the cost.

MR. KILPATRICK: Of the hundreds of major corporations in the country in your judgment not one is doing a good or responsible job—

MR. NADER: Some which are building new plants, are building plants such as in the paper industry, the newer plants are cleaner than the older plants. The reason is that somebody in the corporation made the judgment that it is better and cheaper to invest in the installation of the new plant to control pollutants than to have to be forced to do it by Government five or ten years later when it can be much more expensive.

MISS MOUAT: I would like to carry on with that same theme for a moment. Your critics say that you are inclined not to admit to any progress on the part of corporations or Government agencies. Does this ruin the credibility of the consumer movement, to give a few pats on the back occasionally, or why is this—do you agree with the thesis, first of all?

MR. NADER: First of all, we have given credit where credit is due. We have seen some improvement in the work of the Federal Trade Commission and in a number of instances other regulatory agencies who have done things that they should have done years ago, but they have at least done them now.

Secondly, the point I think is missed. If what you are saying is, could things be worse, you are correct; things could be a lot worse. But we are asking the other question: could things be better, could people have less pollution, could they have greater protection in the integrity of their food products from harmful chemical additives or contaminants? These are all things we are concentrating on. Industry spends hundreds of millions of dollars every year telling the public how great things are, when very often they are not, but we are interested in showing the public how things can be improved.

MISS MOUAT: But you don't think by pinpointing a specific example or two that you can encourage the others to follow suit or you think that has no merit, really, or incentive?

MR. NADER: No, in fact, we are also searching. We pointed out that the National Air Pollution Control Administration was the most open administration in its information policy of all the agencies that we studied, in order to show that the other agencies' restrictive practices were not soundly based. Just a few days ago the Ford Motor Company, largely because of a directive from Henry Ford, turned completely around on the bumper standard and proposed a stronger bumper, to reduce the enormous property damage of four or five miles per hour, to the Department of Transportation. That also was praised as a step forward.

MR. BISHOP: Mr. Nader, on the question of finances, in the past you financed your operations with the help of foundations and some individual businessmen. Now that your targets are larger and broader, are you contemplating any new mechanisms to raise money, such as citizen involvement?

MR. NADER: Yes, as a matter of fact we are launching a national fund-raising drive, appealing to citizens to contribute to a group that we have established, called Public Citizen, in order to carry on our work in a more systematic fashion. That includes the studies of various institutions and the development of techniques and ways by which citizens can have an impact in their community or state or on a national basis.

MR. BISHOP: What are you offering other than that of Common Cause and a number of political organizations who are now starting to raise money for next year's campaign? What precisely are you offering that can't be provided by Common Cause, by political candidates?

MR. NADER: First of all, this does not at all relate to any partisan political purpose, so it is outside of politics. It is going to focus on trying to resurrect the concept of citizenship, which has been given too much avoidance by political institutions. The point is that we can't any longer simply delegate our responsibility as citizens to institutions and vote them in or out every two- or four-year period because things happen in this country daily, not just at election time, and what needs to be done is to forge the kinds of strategies and techniques for citizens' action so that a citizen in a year can be more effective by a great degree than he is now, because the citizen will have a sense of timing, he will know how to get facts, he will know how to develop programs, how to build coalitions and become an effective force.

It really doesn't matter what the particular citizen's opinion is. What we really need is the development of noninstitutional sources of power in the country, so that if citizens come in on a situation, at least they will be making up their minds as citizens, and not on what their employers are expecting them to say or the Government agencies are expecting them to say. In short, a freer source of citizen power.

MR. HACKES: Mr. Nader, your campaign, your GM campaign this year apparently achieved far less than it did last year at the annual meeting. Does this indicate that your drive to reform General Motors is fizzling out?

MR. NADER: No, not at all. It just indicates basically that the large institutional shareholders, like some of the foundations and pension trusts and universities such as Harvard or MIT, have failed utterly to square their statements and their practices. They came out last year and this year with strong statements about GM's lack of responsible management in a number of areas, yet they continually voted for management.

I think what the second year's Campaign GM has shown is that there has to be a far greater energy in having those who are part of these institutions, such as faculty and alumni and students in the university structure decide more closely how these portfolios are going to be voted.

Also, the mutual funds now are being confronted with an SEC statement that they are going to have to let their constituents make certain decisions as to whether, for example, social issues should be part of the mutual fund decision.

I think what the second year campaign did do was to show that it simply isn't enough to make the appeal. There is a lot more work to be done, which I am sure will be done. Beyond that, you can see General Motors already beginning to react to the pressure in some of the things it has done. I think the most promising thing it had done, the one that really isn't cosmetic of all the other things they have done over the last year in response to Campaign GM's pressures, is the naming of Leon Sullivan as the first black director on the board of directors.

MR. HACKES: Looking at it realistically, though, how far can you really expect to go in reforming corporations whose dedication after all is to earning profits for stockholders?

MR. NADER: You see, that is not necessarily inconsistent. What has to be done is to develop a broader calculus of cost so that what corporations now are doing against the public interest because the public is paying for it becomes integrated into their own cost calculations.

For instance, if it is much more costly to continue occupational hazards in foundries or in mines than to eliminate them, because of potential fines, because of lawsuits by the victims, then they are going to change it.

What we simply need to do is to make an inventory of all the impacts that the corporations have on society and ask: Why are the costs not integrated into the costs of doing business? Once they are, then the motivation becomes quite appropriately channeled in the direction of the public interest.

I might also add that harm, when it is not disciplined or controlled, is a competitive advantage, and the honest businessman or the honest industrial practitioner finds that he can't do the right thing because he will be lampooned or harpooned by his particular business competitors. So when the public, whether directly or through Government, establishes certain minima, then the adulteration of food products or cutting corners on pollution will no longer be a competitive advantage.

MR. KILPATRICK: Mr. Nader, some of your fans, many of them, perhaps, have recommended that you make yourself available to be a candidate for President of the United States, and you have responded usually by saying you were less interested in the next President of the United States than in the next President of General Motors.

Which leads me into this question: Would you be interested in a top job in corporate management, yourself?

MR. NADER: No, I wouldn't.

MR. KILPATRICK: Why?

MR. NADER: Because I think I am more effective, and I think there is a far smaller number of candidates for the kind of work that we are doing, which is building up consumer and environmental constituencies among the citizens to keep tabs both on Government and business.

MR. KILPATRICK: You have no interest in partisan politics at all?

MR. NADER: Not all.

MR. KILPATRICK: Never would run for Senate from Connecticut, for example?

MR. NADER: Would not.

MR. KILPATRICK: Let me follow up Mr. Hackes' line of questioning on profits:

Do you take a sort of moralistic view on profits that up

to a certain level they are virtuous and above that they are sinful?

Mr. Nader: Two views. One, an antitrust view, another a moralistic view.

First of all, I think, as we all recognize, the antitrust laws in this country were designed, passed first by a Republican Congress in 1890, to preserve competition and an effective market mechanism.

They are being violated rampantly, epidemically, from price-fixing, to tie-in agreements, reciprocity, down the line. We are going to document that in an 1,100-page report on antitrust enforcement, which will be released next week, for those who are interested in further documentation. So that surplus profits, profits that are obtained because of shared monopolies, or monopolies, or oligopolies are excess profits and as such should not be tolerated by the antitrust laws.

Secondly, there is a moral content. For example, most conservatives would think that a company making money off pornography was not making moral profits. I think a company making money off the infliction of health hazards to people or deceptive practices is not making a moral profit, and I think the moment business gets away from at least paying lip service to that concept, we have lost a basic moral discipline in the business community.

Miss Mouat: Staying with corporations for a moment, an article in today's paper indicated that an employee—well, several employees at General Motors knew of the unsafe mechanical problems in the Corvair at the time of the production, including the president of General Motors, himself, the one who is now the president.

This does raise a question to me, anyway, of how much loyalty does one owe to one's organization and where do you cut the public obligation? Where do you see that line falling?

Mr. Nader: We have given a great deal of thought to that. We think there should be a detailed ethic of whistle blowing. At the moment an individual who works for an organization, whether it is a corporation or a Government agency, surrenders his entire conscience and dignity to the organization's dictates, we have got a Nuremberg problem, and that can be a very, very serious situation. The organization, in effect, is a tyranny where it knows that no matter what it does, it can count on the blind allegiance of the scientists, engineers, lawyers, or assembly-line workers. We have proposed a number of criteria, in a conference that was held early this year, whereby employees would be able to judge at what point have they exhausted their internal remedies, so to speak, and at what point they have to square their conscience with their obligation to their fellow man, which in my judgment, is the first obligation beyond that of the corporation.

MISS MOUAT: Are you also working on protection for the individual if he does do that?

MR. NADER: That is exactly the point. In fact we have an organization on professional responsibility, where this group does receive these kinds of conscience-stricken complaints. We hope to try to help these people and get them legal defense, if necessary.

MISS MOUAT: Let me ask you this: Do you think there are many cases like this, like the GM case, where there is information that is valuable to the consumer which is being withheld, or do you think that the trend of public, outside disclosures is going to continue to be very strong rather than inside?

MR. NADER: I think it will be strong in both areas, but I think there is certainly a pickup on inside disclosure outside, to Government authorities or to consumer environmental groups. The mail that is coming in to our organization on this is increasing, and it shows basically that only the surface has been scratched, that there is a lot of going along by getting along, there are a lot of invisible chains surrounding very well-intentioned employees who just haven't felt that anybody could listen on the outside and could listen and follow through in case they are ostracized or demoted or thrown out of their job.

MR. BISHOP: Mr. Nader, on the one hand you are concerned with institutional reform, the size of institutions, the inertia of large organizations. On the other you spend a considerable time lobbying for this new Consumer Protection Agency. My question is, why will this new large agency, an amalgamation of all the Federal consumer functions, not run into the same problems that large institutions have in the past? Why will this be different, in your opinion?

MR. NADER: I have given a good deal of thought to that point because we have seen too many agencies just develop into bureaucracies captured by those it is supposed to regulate. I think the significant difference is that the proposed independent consumer agency, proposed by Senator Ribicoff in the Senate, Congressman Rosenthal in the House, will have no regulatory function, which incidentally is why it is so vigorously opposed by business interests like the United States Chamber of Commerce. The reason is that this agency would simply have top-flight professionals, lawyers, economists, scientists, accountants and others, representing consumer interests before all the other regulatory agencies. If all these regulatory agencies are acknowledgedly part of an adversary legal system, it is time to have somebody on the other side of the aisle representing the consumer, whether it is a pollution standard, a food and drug standard, atomic energy safety standard, or utility standard, or rate-making process. I think that is what will keep it from being a bureaucracy. There is only one way to justify itself: How vigorous an advocate is it for the consumer interest in getting the facts before these decisional bodies and constantly monitoring and exposing these bodies, in fact, taking them to court as the bill provides when the case merits it.

MR. MONROE: We have less than three minutes.

MR. BISHOP: What is the position of the Nixon Administration on this point? They have made some noble speeches about the consumer movement. Do you find them actually taking a firm stand in this, or are they opposing the separate agency?

MR. NADER: I think the Nixon Administration is opposing a separate agency. I think it has opposed much of the meaningful consumer legislation in Congress, because Mrs. Knauer is not running the consumer show. Those who are running the consumer show are Secretary of Commerce Maurice Stans and Peter Flanigan, who is Assistant to the President. I think it is very unfortunate because in many ways these consumer bills will save billions of dollars in terms of much more effective marketplace activity. They will monitor a lot of the fat and bureaucracy in these regulatory agencies, and they will be in accord with at least the pretensions of the Administration. When it comes down to the nitty-gritty, the Administration goes the way of their business sponsors.

MR. HACKES: Referring again, Mr. Nader, to the angry exchange the other day between you and Senator Ted Stevens of Alaska in which you mentioned criminal fraud, criminal negligence, massive thievery and so forth, you were asked by him: "If this is true, why don't you bring it before a grand jury and seek an indictment?"

Your answer was—or your answer indicated that district attorneys don't have the guts to do that. Are you telling us then that the DA's are owned by big business? Could you expand on that? Is there no way that that can be done?

MR. NADER: There is a simple answer to that question. First of all, this was a problem of automotive service frauds and design frauds that had to be handled at the legislative level. You can't file fifty million suits a year through DA's. But second, the whole structure of the district attorney's office, as has been repeatedly observed in many studies, is of very limited resources and very much honed in on crime in the streets and the more widely publicized crime, not in terms of economic crime. To try to make individual executives responsible within corporations is an enormous expenditure of the kind of subpoena power and resources that most DA's don't have, and if they don't have a real courageous concentration on the fact that the economy can be subverted from within, it can be watered down, adulterated and in effect harmed very badly by corporate or economic crime, they are not going to bend the effort. Time and time again cases referred by regulatory agencies through the Justice department to local district attorneys have been given secondary interest, such as food and drug prosecutions.

MR. MONROE: I am sorry to interrupt. Our time is up. Thank you for being with us today on "Meet the Press."

TWO MYTHS AND A PARADOX [3]

EDWARD N. COLE [4]

Ralph Nader and the other consumer representatives have brought considerable pressure to bear on automobile manufacturers to produce safer vehicles and pollution-free motors. But controversial subjects have more than one side. Speaking for the auto makers, Edward N. Cole, president and chief operating officer of General Motors, suggested some of the problems encountered. On February 10, 1972, in the opening address at the GM-sponsored Institutional Investors Conference, he spoke to a selected group of one hundred "thought leaders" representing large institutional investors (banks, universities, and foundations). He revealed his purpose when he announced in his opening sentences: "To help orient you for the talks you will hear and the things you will see, I would like to talk to you for a few minutes about two myths and a paradox." In this statement he was preparing the way for the other speakers on the program. Following Cole were fourteen presentations by staff executives and project leaders from the GM Technical Center. A representative of the public relations department of General Motors stated that the conference was an outgrowth of the feeling "that because of the rapidly changing social climate and technical progress it was imperative that the corporation improve understanding and communications with its investors and interested persons." Large businesses and industries frequently hold meetings of this type as a part of their public relations programs or as a means of keeping their own employees informed.

The reader should note how skillfully the speaker previewed his development when he mentioned that he intended to consider "two myths and a paradox." As he moved along in his development he used these labels as signposts ("the first myth," "a second myth," and so forth). The speech is simply organized and is filled with interesting and effective supporting material.

For much of the day you will be hearing about technology. To help orient you for the talks you will hear and

[3] Delivered at the GM Technical Center, Warren, Michigan, February 10, 1972. Printed in the 1972 *Report on Progress in Areas of Public Concern* (General Motors Corporation). Copy supplied by Paul R. Miller. The printed version was slightly revised from reading copy.

[4] For biographical note, see Appendix.

the things you will see, I would like to talk for a few minutes about two myths and a paradox.

In recent years it has been popular to talk about the rapidity of change—particularly scientific change. It has been said that scientific knowledge doubles every ten years. No doubt it does. One writer has predicted that the rapid change of products and processes will obsolete the work of 60 million Americans in the next generation. Again, this probably is true.

Still others have pointed out that we are shortening the time from scientific breakthrough to market application. Photography took 112 years from invention to application. The telephone took some 56 years . . . radio 35 . . . radar 15 . . . television 12 . . . and transistors 5 . . . but laser rays made it from the laboratory to application in only 10 months.

If all this is true—and it is—doesn't this mean that new technology in the automobile industry can move in months from the laboratory to the assembly plant and the production of 8.5 million cars a year in the United States?

Absolutely no . . . and that is the first myth. Automotive breakthroughs cannot be translated quickly into production cars. Production lead time, intensive testing, customer acceptance, and cost-benefit analysis determine what and when innovations can be safely and effectively added.

Automotive developments are coming fast. But unlike other products, they apply to very complex products involving safety, health, and the commerce and life of communities. They apply to millions of vehicles requiring a high degree of uniformity, reliability and long life. Both because of the products, their volume and nature of their materials, the manufacturers are faced with expensive tooling and space and manufacturing problems. These characteristics make every automotive decision a major investment and every investment a commitment for several years.

The automobile industry is highly competitive. A wrong engineering decision may affect not only one model, but by creating or destroying customer loyalty, it may affect product success for several years. Every change must go through careful cost-benefit analysis—establishing the priorities for the customers' dollars.

Currently, the industry is in the process of developing an energy-absorbing bumper. In the customers' interest, very detailed studies have been made—such as, the nature and frequency of various types of accidents, the cost of accident repair, and, of course, the costs of the bumper systems themselves. These have been related to the savings that motorists might reasonably expect from reduced insurance premiums. The cost-benefit results are interesting.

The owner of a car with a bumper system that provides protection to all safety-related components at front and rear barrier impact speeds of 5 mph (as required by Federal regulations for 1974 models) would have to wait over 8 years to recover his bumper investment—*if* the premium is reduced 10 percent, or over 5 years *if* the premium is cut 20 percent.

Taking it one step further, if legislation should require a damage-free bumper system that could absorb a 10 mph crash into a barrier on the front and rear—and this is advocated by some state legislators—the average motorist would probably never recover his additional investment through insurance savings alone, *even if he drove his car for 10 years.*

There is another reason why it is a myth to expect automotive developments to be instant additions to automobiles.

The automobile industry depends not only on *research* and *development* but also on long and careful *demonstration* before cars are put in the hands of customers. This is a necessity because of the nature of the products, their use, and the requirements of Federal standards. Customers do not want to be guinea pigs for research—and they shouldn't be.

New developments must work not only under the controlled conditions of the laboratory, but also in the subzero of northern Montana winters and in the high temperatures and high humidity of Florida. They must be engineered and tested for a variety of drivers and for frequently casual or no maintenance.

The timing of Federal standards does not always take into consideration all the essential time factors involved in the development, testing, production, and use of innovations demanded of the automobile industry by those standards.

First, there is the time it takes to develop the new equipment from engineering specifications to laboratory performance under carefully controlled conditions.

Then, after the new device has been tested and retested and refined sufficiently for production, the machinery has to be ready to mass-produce it. Some federally-required innovations are highly sophisticated items—emission control systems, for example, and some day, perhaps, air cushions. They require sophisticated production equipment, which takes time to develop, build, and teach people to operate.

Back in the days when we had more control over the lead time preceding the introduction of new equipment, we could phase it into production. Innovations like power brakes and power steering were first produced at lower volume levels since they were available only as options on certain models. We could proceed with care and caution. Our "learning curve" was more gradual. But today, it is greatly accelerated.

Crash programs can shorten the lead time preceding mass production of some items, but they can also increase the risk of error, especially with complex equipment. In our development work on air cushions, for example, we are very conscious of our liability as a manufacturer. When you are dealing with explosive devices—which air cushions are—you want to know the answers to a lot of touchy questions, such as:

What is the life expectancy of these systems?

What will happen when the vehicle equipped with an air cushion is scrapped?

What is the manufacturer's liability if the cushion deploys and causes an accident? Or if it doesn't deploy quickly enough?

Our first concern, of course, is for the safety of our customers, but, if we are required by law to provide certain equipment to the public at a certain time, we would be remiss if we did not very seriously consider our risks and liabilities as the manufacturer of that equipment.

Our risk and liability consideration are important in the emissions control area as well as in safety. For example, the Clean Air Act, as amended in 1970, requires that emissions control systems be effective for five years or 50,000 miles. There is a recall provision for cars that fail to meet these regulations for the required period—*provided that they have been maintained in accordance with the manufacturer's recommendations.*

To protect ourselves against excessive risk, it will be necessary for us to recommend that these cars be maintained as if they were being operated by owners who give them the hardest use—the two or three percent who drive at the highest speeds, over the worst roads, in the most severe weather.

This will not please the average owner. We have no alternative under the provisions of this law as it stands today, however, because we have not found a way to simulate all the various kinds of use and misuse that a car will get over a five-year period. We can run a car 50,000 miles in about three and one half months, operating around the clock. But we just do not know how to give a car five years of all kinds of driving, weather, road conditions, and maintenance in a relatively short test period.

There is a second myth I would like to mention. Several years ago an idea was widely promoted that there are two worlds—a world of science and technology on one hand and a world of humanism on the other. The two worlds have two languages and very different objectives and goals.

There is a grain of truth in that theory, but only a grain. In industry, the two-world concept is a myth. The worlds of science and nonscience come together in the common objectives of a company. Industry takes the theory of the laboratory and translates it into the practical hardware of the marketplace. It provides motivation for individuals with a variety of talents. They do talk the same language—when they have the common goals of improved service and products for customers.

We do recognize that there has been a problem of language, but it is not so much within a company, as it is between the progress of technology and the understanding of the public. Frequently, technology has moved faster than the public has been able to keep up with it.

For example, judging by our mail and the press, many still feel that the car is the major contributor to air pollution. They believe that the nation's air pollution problem would disappear overnight if we turned off the ignition of every car, truck, and bus in America. Careful studies by several competent researchers show that this is not true. If all cars, trucks, and buses were parked, we would still have 60 percent of our air pollution problem measured by weight, and about 90 percent of the problem as it relates to health. The public has not realized that the automobile's percent of the air pollution problem has been reduced—even though the car population has increased.

These points have been emphasized in literature and on public platforms, but we continue to have a language problem or, perhaps more accurately, a credibility problem. More than ever in the history of our country we need the factual, objective findings of technology as a basis of discussion and decision. To this extent there is a language problem.

In addition to the two myths of instant progress and two worlds, there is also an important paradox that we must recognize. Technology is both a cause and a cure—a saint and a sinner, depending on how it is directed. Critics have pointed out that technology has polluted our environment. It has wastefully used our natural resources, and created an impersonal, mechanistic society.

No one would deny that in many cases this has been true.

As a result, some critics have even insisted that we return to a simpler life . . . that we turn back the clock to the agrarian society of one hundred years ago, reduce our consumption and Gross National Product, and set a goal of zero growth.

Do they want to go back to the days before the Salk vaccine for the prevention of polio? Do they want to do without modern bathrooms, telephones, electricity or other modern conveniences? Would they be willing to go back to the hand-cranked car with two-wheel brakes and boiling radiator, or even further back to the horse and wagon? The answer is not to stop technology but to redirect it with new environmental assignments. Technology can do the job. It can protect and restore our environment, and it can do it to whatever degree the public and the customer want it done. Or, putting it more accurately, to the degree they are willing to pay the cost.

Technology, in itself, is neither good nor bad. It does what people direct it to do. Today you will hear about some of GM's directed technology, directed for the improvement of our environment as well as the benefit and convenience of GM customers.

SOME CONTEMPORARY ISSUES

MURDER AND GUN CONTROL [1]

GEORGE EDWARDS [2]

"For too long we have indulged the gun maniacs. The name of the game is human life and it is a game we dare not play. The stakes are too high for an advanced society which values human life above all other considerations," said Patrick V. Murphy, police commissioner of New York City (see REPRESENTATIVE AMERICAN SPEECHES: 1970-1971, pages 123-9). This statement expresses the feeling of many Americans who abhorred the assassinations of John F. Kennedy, Robert F. Kennedy, and Martin Luther King, Jr., and the increase of crime in the streets. Some states such as New York have attempted to regulate ownership of firearms, but they have had difficulty enforcing these laws because of importation from outside (see Robert Sherrill, "The Saturday Night Special and Other Hardware," New York *Times,* October 10, 1971). In many states there are few restrictions on the purchase and possession of deadly weapons, and what laws exist are not enforced. To make matters more difficult, in December 1971 the United States Supreme Court in a five-to-two decision weakened the Federal Firearms Act which made it a felony to "receive, possess, or transport in interstate commerce . . . any firearms." The language of the act was declared to be ambiguous.

Advocates of strict regulation of handguns have some dramatic statistics to support their arguments. Probably there are 30 to 60 million revolvers and pistols in private hands. FBI statistics show that since 1963 gun homicides have increased 124 percent, while killings by other means increased by 48 percent. One study in Chicago reveals that homicides by firearms increased three times faster than by all other means between 1965 and 1970. Experts estimate that in a single year 100,000 to 200,000 robberies and 8,000 murders will involve pistols and revolvers.

[1] Delivered at the 12th annual meeting of the American Psychiatric Association, Washington, D.C., May 3-7, 1971. In a slightly revised form this speech was published in *American Journal of Psychiatry,* 128(1972), 811-14. Copyright 1972, the American Psychiatric Association. Quoted by permission.

[2] For biographical note, see Appendix.

In light of such facts as these, and aware of public alarm, Judge George Edwards, former police commissioner of Detroit, had a timely topic for his address to the twenty-fourth annual meeting of the American Psychiatric Association, Washington, D. C., May 3-7, 1971. The speech is excellent in many respects. First, the speaker has taken what might have been a dull statistical recital and made it into an interesting and moving presentation. Second, he skillfully establishes his right to speak on his subject. Third, he presents a well-reasoned case with clearly phrased arguments and abundant supporting evidence. His reliance upon causal reasoning deserves the reader's attention. Furthermore he carefully identifies his sources. The student debater will do well to analyze how Judge Edwards puts together an excellent argumentative speech.

In the United States in 1971 the topic of gun control and the topic of murder are inseparable. This speech could properly be called "Four Myths About Murder." They are:

> 1) That present conditions in this country justify the average citizen in living with a top priority fear of being murdered
>
> 2) That most murderers are premeditated killers for money
>
> 3) That the most likely murderer is a stranger—particularly one of another race
>
> 4) That you can protect yourself from murder by keeping a pistol handy

None of these myths is true.

The statistical chance of being murdered in any year is approximately one in 20,000. You can compare that to the chance of being killed in an automobile accident, which is one in 4,000.

The great majority of murders are products not of cupidity, but of high emotion. Anger, fear and jealousy are leading factors.

The great majority of murders are committed by someone closely related to or associated with the victim.

The possession of a handgun greatly increases the possibility that you or someone you love will be killed with or as a result of that weapon.

All present public opinion surveys indicate that fear of criminal attack and homicide is rampant in the mind of our urban dwellers. Such fear may indeed be the most destructive single force in the deterioration of the American city. Yet of all the causes of death, murder is an infinitesimal percentage, and even if we chose to deal only with violent death, criminal homicide rates as one of the smaller of the causes.

Automobile accidents, for example, cause five times as many violent deaths as does homicide. Home and industrial accidents cause two and one half times as many. Falls cause twice as many, and more than twice as many people commit suicide as are killed by the willful act of another. Almost as many people die by fire each year in these United States as are murdered, and very nearly as many people die by drowning to name just two other risks in our daily lives to which few of us ever give more than a passing thought.

Arthur Conan Doyle was one of my favorite authors as a boy. I read everything he wrote that I could lay my hands on—not the least of these being the Sherlock Holmes stories. But his detective novels and those of his successors gave me very poor preparation for what I was later to see of murder in real life. Six years as a trial judge, thirteen years as an appellate judge, and two years as police commissioner of Detroit have given me some very vivid contact with the crime called murder. There is almost no resemblance between ordinary murder as seen in the courts and the average murder mystery.

The murder-mystery writer hypothesizes a single evil malefactor who concocts a long-range plot to kill an innocent party for his (or her) money. There may be such murders. But I have had somewhat vivid contact with perhaps a thousand murders without ever seeing one which fits the pattern. The closest to this pattern in our day, of course, are the gangland executions of the Mafia. But here the evil purpose is sustained by numbers of conspirators and enforced by the discipline of the mob.

Most murder in real life comes from a compound of anger, passion, intoxication and accident—mixed in varying portions. The victims are wives, husbands, girlfriends, boyfriends, prior friends or close acquaintances (until just before the fatal event). The quarrels which most frequently trigger murders might well result in nothing more than bloody noses or a lot of noise, absent a deadly weapon—handy and loaded.

All the statistics show that if you choose with care the people who will share your bedroom with you or your kitchen, or the adjacent bar stool, you will improve your chances from one in 20,000 to one in 60,000.

As for the one third of murders committed by strangers, the overwhelming motive is robbery. Murder generally results from resistance and surprise. Police recommendations in every city are unanimous in counseling against a holdup or burglary victim attempting resistance. Reaching for a gun is the most dangerous possible gesture when confronted by an armed felon. Outside of the movies, there are few people who win in trying to draw when someone else has a gun in his hand.

Much of the current fear of being assaulted and killed by a stranger involves racial fears. Actually in the overwhelming majority of homicides the victim and the assailant are of the same race. Marvin Wolfgang put it this way in his book *Crime and Race:*

National and official crime statistics do not provide data, but enough research has been conducted to permit the definite statement that criminal homicide, like most other assaultive offenses, is predominantly an intragroup, intraracial act. In a detailed five-year study of homicides in Philadelphia (1948-1952), it was noted that in 516, or 94 percent, of the 550 identified relationships, the victim and offender were members of the same race. Hence, in only 34, or 6 percent, of these homicides did an offender cross the race line: 14 were Negro victims slain by whites and 20 were whites slain by Negroes.

Nothing which I have said to this point is designed to minimize the problem of criminal homicide which we face in this country. We have a murder rate over ten times that of Great Britain—and as we will see, since the mid-1960s it has been increasing. I believe deeply in the sanctity of human life and in the duty of our country to guard and protect its citizens. But the mythology of murder has occasioned all too many people purchasing arms as a means of self-defense when in fact such measures greatly increase the hazard to them and their loved ones.

This brings me directly to the topic of gun control.

During the past three and one half years I have served as a member of the National Commission on Reform of Federal Criminal Laws. Recently this Commission sent its Final Report to the President and to Congress. The report deals, of course, with the whole of the criminal law and must be judged on more than just its recommendations on the most controversial topics. There was a substantial minority of the Commission which opposed any new gun-control laws. But this is what the report says concerning the majority position on gun control:

[A] majority of Commissioners recommend that Congress:
1) ban the production and possession of, and trafficking in, handguns, with exceptions only for military, police and similar official activities; and
2) require registration of all firearms.
Among the arguments supporting the majority view are the following. Crimes of violence and accidental homicides will be markedly reduced by suppression of handguns, which, on the one hand, are distinctively susceptible to criminal and impetuous use, and, on the other hand, are not commonly used for sporting purposes as are long guns. State control is ineffective because of differing policies and leakage between states. A comprehensive and uniform registration law will facilitate tracing a firearm when it has been used for criminal purposes.

The working papers of the National Commission on Reform of Federal Criminal Laws and the staff report of the Commission on the Causes and Prevention of Violence contain some compelling data concerning the relationship between murder and handguns:

1) Between 1962 and 1968 sales of long guns doubled while sales of handguns quadrupled (10 million sold in the last decade). Also note that since 1963 homicides involving firearms have increased 48 percent, while homicides by other means have risen only 10 percent.

2) Handguns are the predominant weapon in crime, although they comprise only 27 percent of firearms in the country. Of crimes involving firearms, handguns are used in 76 percent of homicides, 86 percent of aggravated assaults and 96 percent of robberies.

3) The commission studied three major areas of crime: homicide, robbery and aggravated assault. They found that: "Two out of every three homicides, over a third of all robberies, and one out of five aggravated assaults are committed with a gun, usually a handgun."

4) Regarding homicides, they observe that firearms are "virtually the only weapon used in killing police officers," and that handguns have been involved in eight of the nine assassination attempts on Presidents or presidential candidates.

5) Nineteen sixty-six data shows that the rate of accidental firearms deaths by geographic region parallels the pattern of firearm ownership. Over half of firearms accidents involving fatalities occur in or around the home, and about 40 percent of the victims are children or teen-agers.

6) Firearms were used in 47 percent of all completed suicide attempts.

7) The fatality rate of the knife (the next most frequently used weapon) is about one fifth that of the gun. A rough approximation would suggest that the use of knives instead of guns might cause 80 percent fewer fatalities.

No one who fairly contemplates the criminal carnage which occurs in the United States can fail to conclude that disarming the criminal element of our population is essential to our civilization. National statistics indicate that over 6,000 homicides occur in the United States each year with the use of firearms. Yearly we produce a murder rate more than ten times that of England—and that of many other European countries. I know of no way by which we can achieve disarming the criminal or the criminally inclined without accepting the flat prohibition of some weapons and the sale and use of others under some regulation.

The theory believed by many that as a nation we cannot legally accomplish reasonable firearm control because of the Second Amendment to the Constitution is simply not valid. The language of the amendment and its historic interpretation in the courts is not nearly as restrictive as is popularly believed.

The Second Amendment provides: "A well regulated Militia, being necessary to the security of a free State, the right of people to keep and bear Arms, shall not be infringed."

The basic United States Supreme Court interpretation of this amendment came in *United States v. Miller*, 307 U.S. 174, from which we quote the holding in the opinion of Mr. Justice McReynolds:

> In the absence of any evidence tending to show that possession or use of a "shotgun having a barrel of less than eighteen inches in length" at this time has some reasonable relationship to the preservation or efficiency of a well regulated militia, we cannot say that the Second Amendment guarantees the right to keep and bear such an instrument. Certainly it is not within judicial notice that this weapon is any part of the ordinary military equipment or that its use could contribute to the common defense. *Aymette v. State*, 2 Humphreys (Tenn) 154, 158.
>
> The Constitution as originally adopted granted to the Congress power—"To provide for calling forth the Militia to execute the Laws of the Union, suppress Insurrections and repel Invasions; To provide for organizing, arming, and disciplining, the Militia, and for governing such Part of them as may be employed in the Service of the United States, reserving to the States respectively, the Appointment of the Officers, and the Authority of training the Militia according to the discipline prescribed by Congress." With obvious purpose to assure the continuation and render possible

the effectiveness of such forces the declaration and guarantee of the Second Amendment were made. It must be interpreted and applied with that end in view. *United States v. Miller,* 307 U.S. 174, 178.

From this case (and other leading cases, such as *United States v. Tot,* 131 F.2d 261 [3d Cir. 1942], Goodrich, J; *Cases v. United States,* 131 F.2d 916 [1st Cir. 1942], and *Velazquez v. United States,* 319 U.S. 770 [1943] (these two conclusions follow:

First, the prohibition of the Second Amendment has been held to apply only to the Federal Government and not to the states.

Second, the right to carry arms is applicable to the sort of arms which "a well regulated militia" would carry.

While rifles and shotguns have legitimate relationship to the Second Amendment and have legitimate value for both hunting and home defense, handguns suitable for concealment are basically the weapons of the assassin, not of the militia.

Acquaintance with this problem as a judge, as a former police commissioner of the City of Detroit, as a former infantry officer, and at least an occasional hunter convinces me that these three steps should be taken to lessen our criminal carnage:

1) The manufacture and sale and possession of handguns suitable for concealed weapons should be prohibited by state and Federal law.

2) The purchase and possession of rifles or shotguns should in my judgment be a matter of right for any law-abiding citizen. Such weapons should, however, be registered under state law and sold only on proper identification.

3) Interstate mail-order sale or delivery of firearms of any kind should be banned by Federal law.

Let me close by telling the poignant story of my own home town of Detroit where the present Mayor (Mayor Gribbs) has just proposed a tough gun-control ordinance.

I was police commissioner of Detroit in 1962 and 1963. In those two years we watched murder figures with alarm at the possibility they might exceed one hundred. We did not know when we were well off. In the next few years race tensions increased markedly for reasons too long to tell here. In four years, starting in 1965, gun registrations in Detroit quadrupled.

In six years, starting in 1964, murders in Detroit more than tripled, from 138 to 488. Concerning these figures Inspector Delore L. Ricard, head of the Detroit Police Department's Homicide Bureau, said:

There are more homicides in the city because there are more handguns in the city.

The relationship is that clear. You can't go by the increase in registrations, either. The bulk of handguns used in violent crime are not registered.

These were not Conan Doyle type murders. Inspector Ricard also said:

It usually involves people who know each other well or members of of the family. They are sitting around somewhere—a home, a bar—and there is an argument.

Suddenly someone has a gun in his hand. Then someone else is dead.

The argument doesn't have to be important. Maybe it's about cards or politics or even baseball. I can show you homicides that were committed for reasons you could not believe.

Gun accidents increased too. The Violence Commission found that in 1967 more homeowners were killed in gun accidents than had been killed by burglars or robbers in the home over the previous four and one half years.

The problem spilled over into the suburbs too. In Dearborn handgun registrations tripled between 1967 (the year of the Detroit riot) and 1969. During those years the Dearborn police were advertising instructions for women on the use of handguns. From 1967 to 1969 the homicide rate in Dearborn went from zero to an all-time high of seven.

The Violence Commission report provides us with this summary:

> In our urbanized society, the gun is rarely an effective means of protecting the home against either the burglar or the robber; the former avoids confrontation, the latter confronts too swiftly. Possession of a gun undoubtedly provides a measure of comfort to a great many Americans. But the data suggest that this comfort is largely an illusion bought at the high price of increased accidents, homicides, and more widespread illegal use of guns.

Justice Oliver Wendell Holmes once remarked, "Taxes are the price we pay for civilization." In the seventies in this country gun control may well be the price we have to pay for civilization.

EARTH BENEFITS FROM SPACE
AND SPACE TECHNOLOGY [3]

WERNHER VON BRAUN [4]

Pressing problems on the domestic front have caused many persons to question the wisdom of pouring millions of dollars into space technology. They have argued that domestic problems such as poverty, pollution, prison reform, education, transportation, and slum clearance should have priority over the projects of the National Aeronautics and Space Administration (NASA). Budgets have been cut, and the present commitment comes up for review in 1973. In recent months space advocates have become much more active in attempting to answer their critics.

With this object in mind, Dr. Wernher von Braun, former deputy associate administrator of NASA, gave the keynote address on March 13, 1972, at the Goddard Memorial Symposium, an event sponsored annually by the American Astronautical Society. The theme of the meeting was "The Transfer of Space Technology to Community and Industrial Activities." The audience was composed of one hundred top executives from aerospace and related industries.

The speaker, a world-renowned scientist who played a major role in the development of the space program, is a leading authority on his subject. John P. Donnelly, assistant administrator for public affairs of NASA, says, "Dr. von Braun (like virtually all the other executives I know that must carry . . . enormous workload and responsibilities) receives some staff assistance, primarily research." The speech is well conceived, organized, and constructed. It presents an effective argument for space technology.

We are here to explore the relevance of aerospace technology to industry and the community. It is not an easy assignment.

[3] Delivered to the Goddard Memorial Symposium, March 13, 1972, at Hilton Hotel, Washington, D.C. Permission to print granted by John P. Donnelly, assistant administrator for public affairs, National Aeronautics and Space Administration.

[4] For biographical note, see Appendix.

One of the most difficult tasks is to demonstrate for public understanding the relationship between a vigorous aerospace industry and the national economy, between American leadership in aerospace science and technology and America's high standard of living.

The major contributions to our standard of living by the areospace industry are not felt directly by the bulk of our population, and therefore are not identified with the industry. Even more remote are the effects of large Federal programs in developing aerospace science and technology which are basic to the industry's activities.

Superficially, it is deceptively easy to furnish numerous examples of innovations from aerospace programs which have entered nonaerospace fields of medicine, commerce, business, industry and education. The list is impressive. But, individually, and scattered throughout the economy, they make little or no impression on the public.

It is even harder to measure precisely the intangible gains from space activities in terms of national prestige, spirit, and life concepts. Yet the achievements in space have contributed significantly to all of these things. It is impossible to put numbers on these abstractions, but they may be the most important legacies of our activities in space.

One of the problems of informing Americans of the very real contributions made by the space program is the lack of visible, direct links between what we spend on space activities, and any important gains for society. There are literally no tangible, direct benefits that are *visible* to Americans which seem important.

We can talk all we want to, for example, about the important scientific and technological capabilities we are creating for the nation—capabilities which are basic to much of what the public wants done—and it means exactly nothing. People do not relate science and technology to the everyday business of living, fighting the daily traffic, and buying the groceries. If they do, they are apt to cuss it.

We can point in vain to communications and weather satellites which are revolutionizing worldwide telephone, television and weather-forecasting techniques. People simply yawn. They rarely if ever phone Europe or Japan, they can still catch the ball game on TV, and they still get caught in snowstorms.

So, who needs the space program?

In this symposium, we are addressing ourselves to a narrower discussion of space technology transfer to community and industrial activities. Yet, I would hope that some thought for public understanding of the subject matter will be included in the presentations, for that is the ultimate aim of these deliberations.

Almost two years ago, Dr. William D. McElroy of the National Science Foundation told a House committee that "civilized man cannot long survive on this planet without increased creation of new knowledge and its enlightened use."

He added that the best means to insure continued support of basic science and its smooth transition to applications were the mission-oriented agencies.

Dr. McElroy was speaking for the need of a sweeping reevaluation of science and technology and their roles in society. But he could have been describing the broad role of large NASA programs, such as Apollo and the manned space shuttle. NASA is a mission-oriented agency. Its programs, like Apollo and the shuttle, focus the energies, the brains and imaginations of large numbers of talented people working in all the disciplines in a concerted, coordinated effort which advances science and technology over a broad front. NASA grants have supported research for a broad body of basic studies, and our scientific spacecraft have telemetered back to Earth vast quantities of basic data on phenomena of the solar system and universe. Returns from the Apollo lunar explorations are so great that it will be years before we will know its full value to mankind, but already the increase to our knowledge and understanding is priceless.

These contributions alone go a long way to justify the space program. But the benefits to be derived are largely in the future, whereas the public is more sensitive and responsive to the here and now. Many examples exist of space technology adapted to nonspace use, but the significance of almost all of this has had little visible effect in the public consciousness.

Of course, we all expected it would be a little while before our space activities brought benefits easily identified as important in the public eye. What we did not foresee among future "benefits" was that Apollo would arouse a new, more Utopian concept of what government can do to improve the quality of life here and now on Earth. Demands and expectations for immediate improvements in society are on a scale which considerably exceed the cost of a manned expedition to Mars.

Ironically, in the general clamor to reorder national priorities, NASA—far from being credited for this service—found itself relegated to a level of decreased budgets.

Our difficulty is that as a nation of short-term pragmatists, Americans are not geared mentally to long-range planning and deferred benefits from advanced science and technology programs.

The coming decade may see some shift in the public attitude and a growing awareness of the contributions of space, however, as applications of technology from NASA programs gain prominence. Space technology has a substantial value to the nonaerospace field. We all know it, but the problem is to get the public to know it. The simple fact is America has built its strength and its standard of living on its leadership in technology. In the past two decades or so, our high productivity in high-technology products has kept us ahead of the competition from abroad. The only way to stay ahead is to continue to invest in our high-technology—producing aerospace programs.

A glance at our big foreign trade surpluses tells why. The excess of annual US exports over imports is in high-technology products, such as aerospace, running at $3.6 billion; computers, at $1.1 billion; and machinery, $1.0 billion.

Just the reverse is shown by our low-technology products. Motor vehicle imports over exports are $3.3 billion, followed by clothing and textiles, $1.9 billion, and iron and steel, $1.9 billion.

I think these illustrations indicate quite clearly which side our bread is buttered on: we are strongest in high-technology, and weakest in low-technology competition. American leadership in aerospace research and development has given us a world market in products which require constant advances in high technology and high productivity, activities in which we have excelled for a generation or more.

In the low-technology fields, however, where products can be produced by cheaper labor, the competitive advantage lies with foreign industry where wages are lower. Although this country is the leading motor car producer in the world, for example, the bulk of our car market is within the United States, and export sales abroad meet stiff competition. Foreign car manufacturers, however, are increasingly building up their sales here because they are competing against labor costs, not high technology.

The importance of what we do in aerospace technology may be lost on some Americans who find it hard to relate their everyday lives to space projects and activities. But there can be little doubt that economically our standard of living depends upon our maintaining vigorous programs in developing aerospace science and technology.

This is the broad picture of the benefits coming out of our aerospace programs and industry. I think it is extremely important that we Americans gain an understanding of how basic the development of high technology—especially high aerospace technology—is to our standard of living.

Every industrially capable foreign country is ambitious to penetrate the lucrative markets our high technology has developed, of which the domestic American market is the prime target. Already there is a rising tide of competition from overseas in electronics, aircraft, instruments and controls, telecommunications, and others. It isn't hard to see where this trend will lead if we permit it. The only alternative visible—and I think you will agree that it is a most undesirable one—is for Americans to reduce wage levels so that we are competitive with overseas labor in the low-technology areas.

Now let's look at some other benefits of space and space technology.

Space exploration has made a real impact on astronomy. Historically, astronomy has played a key role in the development of civilization for thousands of years, in agriculture, geography and navigation. In later times, astronomy has figured in a welter of discoveries in the physical sciences and their experimental tools—including optics, spectroscopy, specialized photography and infrared techniques. Traditionally also, astronomy has served to advance mathematics and philosophy.

Space technology has now added a new dimension to astronomy by providing better observation of celestial objects through the elimination of atmospheric refraction and systematic errors. Benefits range from a large number of new discoveries in planetary physics, geophysics, and the chemical and physical properties of the solar system and the galaxies beyond.

All these discoveries are changing our concepts of the universe and man's place in it profoundly. Concepts of man and the universe, and man in the universe, motivate our thinking and actions on Earth. Are contributions to such concepts unimportant to the quality of life Americans strive for today? On the contrary, I think they are basic to the definition of what we mean about quality in life. Without a growing precision of our definition of the universe and its elements, we cannot hope to improve more than the physical aspects of day-to-day living; predictably, life would then soon degenerate into crass materialism.

So, by providing spacecraft to carry the astronomer's instruments and telescopes, the space program is contributing to the fundamental welfare and betterment of mankind. True, these are long-term contributions. They will not directly put food in our mouths, roofs over our heads, or clothes on our backs. But surely no one will say they are unimportant, that we can put off acquiring the abstract benefits of space astronomy indefinitely because of more "urgent" problems. Is materialism our most urgent requirement?

The correct answer, I believe, must be to supply both our material and conceptual requirements simultaneously—sufficient to the physical welfare of people and the growth of cosmology and the sciences.

In the area of technological innovation or spinoff, some of which will be discussed here today and tomorrow, there have been major civilian applications that are now in commercial development. NASA has described many thousands of other potentially commercial space-program developments which are available for use. However, because the time cycles of orthodox American industry—from invention in the laboratory to the appearance of a product on the market—range anywhere from ten to twenty-five years, only a relative few examples of transfers have been documented.

In the medical field, there have been individual instrument- and equipment-transfers that are particularly impressive. These range from improvement in X-ray diagnostics and physiological sensors to special equipment for handicapped patients, and a widening use of remote monitoring of hospital patients.

Some contributions from the space program occur when research spurs consolidation within a field by developing an application for known technology not previously used in that manner. One such contribution, in fluid dynamics, was the consolidation of technology in very low pressure devices for control systems. A machine tool manufacturer noted its significance and studied it for use as a control principle in operating automatic turret lathes. A prototype proved successful, and the company has built these machines in three sizes. They have been sold in a price range of $35,000 to $75,000 each.

The petroleum industry has been aided by technology directly resulting from space research. High-quality color photographs of the Earth taken by our astronauts have helped locate potential oil-producing sources. Navigation via satellite has allowed marine explorers to fix their positions regardless of the weather. Airborne multispectral scanners, developed for the Earth Resources program, have provided color imagery of the terrain, permitting identification of different rock types, including oil-producing outcroppings. High-speed gravity-measuring techniques, used in studying lunar gravity, permit faster and less expensive survey of offshore areas. The magnetometer experiments deployed by Apollo astronauts are adding to our knowledge of continental drift which petroleum geologists find of direct interest in their work.

In addition to its contributions to liquefied natural gas carriers in shipbuilding, NASA-generated technology has opened new possibilities for the surgeon in cryogenic surgery. In surgery, cryogenics has been used to treat Parkinson's disease, remove tumors and cataracts, and for bloodless tonsilectomies. Cryogenic superconductivity signals a new generation of motors, computer memory cores, power transformers, magnets and transmission lines.

It now seems that the food industry, facing increasing problems in the use of food additives and nutritional quality, may be able to draw on NASA's extensive knowledge about food processing, preservation, and nutritional value. We have extremely rigid requirements for the food we supply the astronauts since any type of food-system failure would have grave consequences. Food must be free from bacterial contamination; it must be of high, known nutritional value; it must be stable without refrigeration under wide temperature variation for long periods of time; and it must be capable of fast, reliable and foolproof preparation.

The precautions we have taken with food for the astronauts have led to new and improved methods of processing, preserving and sterilizing it. These may have significant value to both the food industry and the consumer. For example, a flour company, responsible for a number of food items for NASA, has developed precooked, prebuttered rolls that are preservable up to 600 days. In another case, a scientist under NASA contract produced an instant rice that is truly "instant." Normal hot tap water (about 155 degree F) can be used, and it takes under three minutes to serve from shelf to table.

Using NASA-developed methods, certain foods can be prepared and stored for emergency situations. If a disaster occurred, the food could be immediately shipped to the stricken area with no loss in preparation time and no need for refrigeration.

Space research and aeronautics, as we all know, have a lot in common. Aeronautics has contributed a great deal to the advance of space systems, and similarly the space effort has reciprocated. One of the most notable examples that comes to mind is the space program's contribution to air navigation.

Before the airlines began populating the skies with ten-mile-a-minute jetliners, precise navigation—while important—was not so critical as it is becoming today. Now, however, thanks to Apollo, airline pilots have available a new navigation aid that gives them instantaneous and continuous position reports. It operates on the same basic principle that enables our Apollo astronauts to pinpoint their positions far out in space. The heart of this system is a computer fed by a series of accelerometers which sense every movement of the airplane, up or down, sideways or forward. The computer translates this data into the instant and continuous position reports required by pilots flying the crowded airways.

The system is self-contained, and therefore independent of radio, radar, weather, and interference. Because it is more accurate than previous navigation devices, it contributes to a shorter flight time and savings in fuel. Only the most modern airliners now have these nav-aids, but the new generation of aircraft being built will employ them widely.

Related to this benefit is another planned navigation aid of an even higher order. NASA, together with the airlines and other Government agencies, has used the applications-technology satellites to demonstrate how a satellite may serve as a space reference point.

We have shown that the satellite can provide position fixes of exceptional accuracy. The planned operational system will be a complementary means of navigation to individual aircraft. In contact with both airplane and land-based stations, the satellite can give the traffic controller an independent means to follow the airliner's progress. Satellite-relayed data can confirm or correct the pilot's position reports, which are based on his onboard equipment.

Today there is profound concern about clean water and clean air. Space technology can play an important role in helping achieve both. Environmentalists may be interested in an advanced type of sensor that measures carbon monoxide concentrations; this device was developed in a program initiated by our Langley Center. The Langley experiment is designed to make global measurements of carbon monoxide over a period of a year in order to map the portions of the atmosphere with high, low and average concentrations of the gas. In this way, scientists hope to identify the so-called removal sinks in which the gas is changed to another compound.

This may help to solve the riddle and explain why the total concentration of the gas in the air is not increasing, although motor car exhausts, industrial activities and other sources generate some 200 million tons of carbon monoxide each year. Scientists have estimated that the atmosphere contains about 500 million tons of carbon monoxide, but measurements over a period of years have not shown appreciable increases. This implies there must be some natural mechanism that removes most of the gas as it is generated. It would aid environmental control efforts to know what the mechanism is and its capacity for converting carbon monoxide to another compound.

In the effort to obtain cleaner water, we have a lightweight precision sensor designed to detect color gradations in water so oceanologists can spot pollution. Called a multichannel ocean color sensor, it is more sensitive to color than the human eye, and will be flown initially on aircraft. Eventually, it may be placed aboard spacecraft for monitoring the oceans. Data it provides can also be used to spot areas where fish are likely to be, and to study marine biology.

Given repetitive exact color information from this device, oceanologists can chart trends in pollution and marine life for use in preserving and developing ocean resources.

The major contribution for environmental uses is, of course, the Earth Resources Technology Satellite, now scheduled to be launched in the first week of June. We believe this may have the greatest potential of all for realizing hard economic returns from space exploration.

Information from the ERTS' battery of sensors will be relayed to an Earth-based, computerized data-handling and -analysis network. In this way, regional data banks all over the world will receive daily volumes of data that can be put to work for man's benefit in three basic directions:

The information will help provide more of everything through far better management of the world's resources.

It will uncover new resources.

It will identify trouble areas so that remedial action can be taken at the earliest possible time.

To give you an idea of the volume of data traffic to be received, the ERTS satellite will relay several hundred million bits of information daily to Goddard. Goddard in turn will produce some 300,000 color, black and white, and digital tape photos of the Earth's surface each week.

Our Skylab, to be launched next spring, will tie into ERTS experiments by supplying complementary information from astronaut-monitored experiments aboard the space station. At the end of each manned visit to Skylab, the astronauts will bring back with them data on photographic film and digital data on magnetic tape. These Skylab experiments will form an important part of the development of instruments and sensors for the ERTS program because the astronauts will monitor their performance.

The space shuttle, however, offers the greatest potential for space benefits over the long term. It will be the first true space transport due to its versatility as a carrier of men and equipment, its flexibility in operations, and its ability to make repeated missions on a routine basis. While the civilian-oriented missions are the most intriguing in NASA's eyes, the Defense department also sees its usefulness in military operations—for the launch and recovery of surveillance satellites, for example.

The shuttle's cargo bay can be used not only to carry a variety of spacecraft to be placed in desired Earth orbit, but also will accommodate a complete laboratory module in which scientists and engineers can conduct experiments under space environmental conditions. In addition to placing spacecraft in orbit, the shuttle can retrieve them for repair, or to install new experiments, and reuse. This means that scientific and other space satellites can be built less expensively than they can at present, because designs need not include such high standards for reliability. More off-the-shelf items can be used, resulting in large dollar- and time-savings.

The space shuttle now planned will be only the forerunner of much more advanced multiple-mission type spacecraft. The knowledge we shall gain from its design, construction and operational performance will teach us a great deal more about such vehicles and their uses. To fully utilize space for the benefit of man, the multiple-mission spaceship is a must.

The work that NASA is doing in advancing science and technology—pushing forward the frontiers of knowledge—cannot be overstated. The vigor with which we carry on the development of science and technology, the spirit with which we explore the unknown, are characteristic of vital, growing nations that will be ready with the answers to problems of the future.

There's a little-known anecdote from history which illustrates the role played by science and technology in the life of a great nation. It appears in Volume 4 of Joseph Needham's *Science and Civilization in China.* It relates how political decisions dimmed and finally extinguished the final blaze of splendor of one of the world's great civilizations.

Needham says that a series of seven expeditions began to explore the seas to the south and west of China in 1405. Under command of Cheng Ho, the fleet carrying 37,000 men reached the town of Malindi in what is now Kenya three quarters of a century before Columbus made his first voyage to America. By 1433, Cheng's fleet had reached Mecca, and by the time he left Africa for the last time the Portuguese had hardly begun to explore the continent's west coast.

Compared with contemporary European ship technology, the Chinese armada was a revelation. Sixty-two of the ships were nine-masted galleons 450 feet long from bow to stern and more than 180 feet in beam. The vessels not only had multiple masts, but also fore-and-aft rigged sails, and true axially mounted rudders. Strong bulkheads divided the hulls into naturally watertight compartments. The Chinese also installed pedal-operated bilge pumps, developed from the principle of the noria used in ancient China to raise water into irrigation channels. These last two items did not appear in European ships until the eighteenth century.

Beside these great ships, Columbus's vessels appear pitiful.

Cheng Ho's expeditions were, however, the last important explorations of the seas made by China. The political decisions that killed them, Needham says, were part of a decisive *turning inward* of China's civilization. Despite China's early and extensive lead over Europe in science and technology, it was not in China that the scientific revolution took place. Yet, a Chinese visitor to England in A.D. 1400 would have considered that country technologically backward.

Let us hope we can learn from history. There have been disquieting signs of an "inward turning" among Americans which we can only hope is but temporary. Carried to the extremes that occurred in China of the middle ages this could be nothing less than a catastrophe to modern America.

Scientifically and technologically, however, we have built the foundations for America's greatest age. Space offers the opportunity to fulfill the requirements of the spirit while we increase our capabilities to meet the material needs of ourselves and fellow men.

THE ENVIRONMENT REVOLUTION [5]

WILLIAM D. RUCKELSHAUS [6]

On January 29, 1972, William D. Ruckelshaus, director of the Environmental Protection Agency (EPA), addressed the fifteenth commemorative session of the Virginia General Assembly, meeting in the reconstructed hall of the House of Burgesses in Colonial Williamsburg. In the years since the former capitol was reopened to the public, in February 1934, the assemblymen have periodically come to this historic place for commemorative meetings. In addition to legislators, justices of the state Supreme Court, members of Congress, the president of the nearby College of William and Mary, and the members of the board of the Colonial Williamsburg Foundation were also present.

The speaker faced the problem of adapting his contemporary subject to a setting rich in history. He works into his presentation many specific references to Virginia and its leaders. Building the development of his speech around the Jefferson quotation concerning "usufruct" is an ingenious device that leads him to the heart of his topic. What he says is not highly dramatic, but it is a good statement of the Nixon Administration's stand on "wise management of our national resources."

Two hundred years ago this House of Burgesses was the setting for some of the most impassioned oratory in the history of the world. It was noble speech, designed to open men's eyes to the glories of a new ethics, a new politics, and a new philosophy of government.

The sentiments expressed therein have since swept the world, and though neither we nor any nation have yet filled the promise of democracy, neither have we forgotten it. We still sail by the stars of justice and equality; opportunity, challenge and change.

Today we face the necessity of making still another revolution, one which must be accomplished not by force of

[5] Delivered to the General Assembly of Virginia, Williamsburg, Virginia, January 29, 1972.

[6] For biographical note, see Appendix.

arms, but by force of intellect. We must recast our thinking to fit the dictates of our age, just as the founding fathers remolded theirs.

Indeed, ours is the more difficult task. Whereas Patrick Henry's foe was the King, our worst enemy is ourselves.

Our ancestors found a virgin continent here; such a plenitude of fish and game, forests and fertile soil that they can be excused perhaps for thinking its treasures inexhaustible. They exploited it and we—their descendants—grew wealthier in terms of income than any other nation in history.

Unfortunately we paid a heavy price for this progress in terms of air and water pollution, exhausted minerals, wasted forests, urban sprawl and the loss of plant and animal species. We tolerated too much noise, congestion and plain ugliness.

It was man against himself, slowly undermining the foundations of prosperity and of life itself.

But we can't claim the defense of ignorance of natural law. We had been warned by more than one of the founding fathers against prodigal waste of our soil and woodlands and minerals. Thomas Jefferson, perhaps the best example, was intensely interested in wise management of our natural resources.

Jefferson should be reread today as we take stock of what we have done and left undone in the almost two-hundred-year-old American experiment. Speculating once upon the role of man and his relation to the earth, he said: "The earth belongs always to the living generation. They may manage it then, and what proceeds from it, as they please during their usufruct."

The concept of "doing as we please" has always appealed to us Americans. We expect to live where we please, think as we please, drive where we please. But now we see consequences of mindless license which Jefferson's generation could not even imagine, except on a small scale. We know that man's works can threaten the air, the oceans and even the land itself.

But note that term "usufruct." Under an agreement of usufruct, a tenant may use the fruit of the orchard and the land, but he is bound to preserve the basic resources as they were received. He has the use of the land in his own time, but must pass it on without damage.

So Jefferson saw all generations merely as tenants for a time. Behind his concept of freedom to do as you please was an implicit call for conserving resources and handing them on to the next generation in perpetual husbandry.

I think we have enough time to adopt a new usufruct— new styles of living, working, consuming and recreating— and thereby ensure the welfare of posterity. We can make it if we maximize the built-in advantages of our unique system of federal democracy.

One of the strong points of our tradition is that power is dispersed among the states. True, for the last four decades power has gravitated steadily toward Washington. The states did not have the resources or the will to manage social and environmental problems that were regional and even national in scope. As a former state legislator myself, I have to admit that often we did not act even when we could.

Now this pattern is changing. There is a trend in favor of redispersal of power and problem-solving capacity. The widespread call for participatory democracy is a healthy sign that people are tired of paternalism—they want to take responsibility for their own fate.

Moreover the historic decision of *Baker v. Carr* is gradually restoring new vitality to state governments everywhere. Reapportionment on the basis of "one man—one vote" enables you as legislators to represent more of the urban and suburban reality of modern America. In my opinion, we have come a long way back toward the worthy principle that there shall be no legislation without representation.

State governments all over America are just beginning to feel their new dignity and their new potential. You are seizing new opportunities to solve problems in fields as diverse as consumer protection, pollution abatement, transportation, civil rights and land-use planning.

I might add that the successful outcome of these initiatives will be assisted in no small part by the passage of the President's revenue-sharing bill and the implementation of other aspects of his New Federalism. But you yourselves have a job to do.

Take the water pollution bill now before the House. If this or any similar act should be passed by Congress, you will be given additional responsibilities for controlling effluent discharges and managing the construction of sewage treatment plants.

You will have to greatly augment your pollution enforcement activities. The Federal Government has no ambition to intervene in enforcement but will inevitably do so if the states don't act.

Certainly it is a matter of pride to Virginia that such beautiful and fruitful historic rivers as the Rappahannock and the Shenandoah be cleansed and restored to a semblance of their original condition. These rivers that nourished the Founding Fathers and inspired their intense love of the American landscape should not be allowed to degenerate into ugly, lifeless ditches.

It's bad enough that two rivers in this country are inflammable. Unless we reverse field soon, we are going to wind up with rivers like the Rhine-Meuse in Holland which is so full of chemicals that you can develop film in it.

Of course water pollution control is but one dimension of the environmental challenge which confronts the states. The advent of a new pesticides bill, which has passed the House and pends in the Senate, will mean that these chemicals would be divided into two categories of use—the general and restricted. Those designated as restricted would require trained applicators licensed by the state. Each state would have to establish an apparatus to enforce the provisions of the bill.

Moreover, in coming years you are going to be more heavily involved in the mounting problems of solid-waste disposal. We in EPA are financing a number of experimental trash-disposal techniques and we are helping close down five thousand open dumps which threaten public health. But only you in the state capitals have the perspective and the authority to set up coordinated, regional solid-waste policies.

Perhaps the most immediate challenge to you as state leaders is finding ways to implement the air-quality standards mandated by the Clean Air Amendments of 1970. The problems of adjustment are different in each state and therefore each must make its own original response. But the problem will not go away and neither will the public's insistence upon workable solutions.

And finally, there is land-use planning. If the President's land-use bill passes you will be obliged to set policy on the location of new communities and control the siting of highway interchanges, airports, shopping centers, office complexes, recreational facilities and colleges.

If the states were ever a backwater in American politics, times certainly have changed. They are now on the front lines in a number of environmental battles, virtually all of which require regional or statewide planning and action.

In this connection I want to express my admiration for the very far-reaching and far-sighted environmental program that has been proposed by Governor Holton. A Department of Natural Resources, along with other steps contemplated, would certainly do much to assure the preservation and wise use of your heritage. Those who wish Virginia well can only hope the governor's proposals will get the most careful consideration.

Indeed, several states already have established natural resource or environmental protection type agencies to formulate a broad, coordinated, and independent approach to environmental problems. Illinois, Maryland, New Jersey, New York, Washington, and Hawaii are among these. A number of other states are currently considering such reorganization.

There is much merit in establishing a central focus of responsibility for the environment, but it should not be done without the clear understanding that every agency of government at every level must exercise its own responsibility for the protection of our common surroundings. No single agency, no matter how well staffed or financed, can alone police the environment and undo the damage of decades.

Moreover, two factors are vital to the success of environmental agencies. First, they must pursue a rigorously independent course. They must not be given a role in promoting agriculture or commerce, but be entrusted only with the singular task of protecting environmental quality.

Second, these agencies must lead and educate as well as regulate. Pollution is not just a government matter, it is society's problem too. As citizens and consumers we have all had a hand in degrading the environment, and now we all share a common duty to restore its natural balances.

We must teach everyone to accept his personal obligations in the web of life, to appreciate the intricate relations among all living things, to realize that man is only one element in a system—dependent on all the other elements for his health, his prosperity and his very life.

The message I would leave with you today is that Washington and the states must work in concert—in a relationship of mutual concern and responsibility. The Federal Government has neither the wisdom, the resources nor the inclination to have it otherwise. There aren't any one-dimensional, one-time solutions that can be imposed everywhere without regard to local conditions.

What, then, is the Federal role?

It is simply to articulate national goals and to set and enforce national standards. The advantage of Federal standards and enforcement is obvious. Every state has to follow through. No state will profit by providing a haven for polluters. No company has any incentive to move from one jurisdiction to another to escape controls. Everyone has to do his share. At the same time, a state can set more stringent requirements, can be even more solicitous of its natural heritage.

As we work together, we must also work effectively. We must employ a unified, total approach to the problems of environmental protection, not the piecemeal, disjointed commitment of previous years. The nature of the problems demands a systems response. And as the consequences of failure would be tragic, our commitment to succeed must be total.

This nation has never lacked for men and women of vision who had more in mind for our natural heritage than using it up, who wanted to conserve the best that we had inherited from the past.

When you look beyond the quaint charm of this historic town you see that it grew from a highly sophisticated design, one perfectly accommodating its surroundings, a model of urban settlement with few parallels even in the great era of town planning in the nineteenth century and none in its own time. This product of civic foresight and pride has been preserved for our own edification by an extraordinarily generous and timely philanthropy.

What Colonial Williamsburg proves to me is that in one sense we do not really have to invent a new environmental ethic. We have only to look to the best thinking of our forebears to see the irresistible course of the future. Indeed, we can also take a lesson from more recent history.

A decade ago this nation set itself the goal of reaching the moon and some day of exploring the mysteries of the universe. Today we propose a more difficult objective, one which requires the conquest of an inner universe of obsolete gratifications.

President Nixon has said these must be the years when America pays its debt to the past by reclaiming the purity of its air, its water, and its living environment. That will demand a rediscovery of certain ancient virtues and forswearing vices equally venerable.

But because we have always been a revolutionary people at heart I have no doubt of the course we shall take. With persistence we can achieve the victory of the best that is in us.

SO BAFFLING A MAN:
A CRITICAL EVALUATION

ROOSEVELT'S PLACE IN HISTORY [1]

ARTHUR SCHLESINGER, JR. [2]

More has probably been written about Franklin D. Roosevelt than about any other American of this century. Each year one or two books about him or his wife Eleanor increase the growing body of Rooseveltiana. In 1970 James MacGregor Burns published *Roosevelt: The Soldier of Freedom,* a sequel to an earlier volume. Currently among the best sellers is Joseph P. Lash's highly lauded *Eleanor and Franklin,* a book mainly about Mrs. Roosevelt. But this outpouring does not seem to exhaust interest in Roosevelt among the general public or among scholars.

For the ninetieth birthday of FDR, January 30, 1972, the Alumni Association of Hunter College arranged a commemorative program entitled "Franklin D. Roosevelt in Retrospect," at Hunter College, New York City. (Hunter has a close connection with the Roosevelts because the family townhouse at 47 East 65th Street was acquired as a meeting center for Hunter College groups.) One of the noteworthy features of the program was the paper read by Professor Arthur Schlesinger, Jr., distinguished historian, author of a three-volume study of Roosevelt, and long-time admirer of the thirty-second President. This presentation gave the historian an occasion to puzzle over his subject, saying: "Still the impenetrability of his nature, the elusiveness of his style, rendered him a hard man to figure out, both when he was alive and after his death."

This paper is an academic lecture prepared for a special occasion. A notable scholar, chosen for his background in the subject, delivers a carefully prepared presentation. He "reads his paper" because he respects the perceptive powers of discriminating and critical listeners. Frequently these papers after delivery become a part of the literature on the subject. The Schlesinger paper is an excellent example of this type of speech.

[1] Delivered at a commemorative program at Hunter College of the City University of New York, New York City, January 30, 1972. Quoted by permission.

[2] For biographical note, see Appendix.

There is nothing more evanescent and unreliable than the verdict of history. For the verdict of history is only the verdict of one generation of historians. Alas, every new generation of historians has its own worries about the future and consequently its own demands on the past; and each tends to recreate the past in the image of its own preoccupations and values. Reputations rise and fall, like stocks on Wall Street, responding to the supply and demand equations of some later age. In addition, as Emerson reminds us, "Every hero becomes a bore at last"—though not necessarily forever; every hero, however out of fashion for a season, also remains a subject for revival. The one certainty in history is the revision of historical judgment. That is why the word "definitive" is employed only by reviewers who do not understand what history and biography are all about.

But the historiographical rhythm is not altogether unpredictable. The reputation of a commanding figure is often at its lowest in the period ten to twenty years after his death. We are always in a zone of imperfect visibility so far as the history just over our shoulders is concerned. It is as if we were in the hollow of the historical wave; not until we reach the crest of the next one can we look back and estimate wisely what went on before. When I went to college in the 1930s, Theodore Roosevelt and Woodrow Wilson were at the nadir of their reputations. Henry Pringle's brilliant but deflationary biography of 1931 had set—it seemed for good —the image of TR as the adolescent-at-large in public affairs; the First World War revisionists had set—it seemed for good —the image of Woodrow Wilson as the man who had misled the United States into a foolish war and then botched the peace. But the passage of time and the emergence of new concerns produce new judgments. Those Theodore Roosevelt stocks have been rising steadily on the historians' exchange; and Woodrow Wilson has long since recovered from the gross disfavor of the thirties, though new generations, it is true, have perceived new flaws in the Wilsonian character and outlook.

The reputation of Franklin D. Roosevelt has undergone particular permutation and vicissitude. This is partly because of the elusive nature of the man. Some men stride into history all of a block, solid, positive, unitary, monolithic, granite-like, impermeable; thus, in our time, Churchill, Stalin, De Gaulle. Others are not blocks but prisms; they are sensitive, glittering, quicksilver, protean, pluralistic; their levels of personality peel off with the delusive transparence of the skins of an onion, always frustrating the search for a hard core of personality within. One recalls Keynes's description of Lloyd George:

. . . rooted in nothing; he is void and without content; he lives and feeds on his immediate surroundings; he is an instrument and a player at the same time which plays on the company and is played on by them too; . . . with six or seven senses not available to ordinary men, judging character, motive, and subconscious impulse, perceiving what each was thinking and even what each was going to say next, and compounding with telepathic instinct the argument or appeal best suited to the vanity, weakness or self-interest of his immediate auditor.

The greatest statesmen, like Lincoln, partake of both qualities, are both granite and prism. FDR, I would judge, was more a fox than a hedgehog. He had, not a single personality, lucid, definite and infrangible, but a ring of personalities, each dissolving on touch, each promising to reveal another beneath, all concealing the central core of personality. Yet it could not be said of Roosevelt, as Keynes said of Lloyd George, that he was rooted in nothing. FDR's paradox lay in the contrast between the dazzling variety on the surface, the succession of masks, so easily donned and doffed, and what one can only feel to be, in the end, a basic simplicity, even innocence, of mind and heart. The complexity, the deviousness, were real enough, but they pertained to tactics. "He sometimes tries to appear tough and cynical and flippant," the really tough and cynical and flippant Harry Hopkins once told Robert E. Sherwood, "but that's an act he likes to put on. . . . You and I are for Roosevelt because he's a great spiritual figure, because he's an idealist." His methods were often tricky, but they did not corrupt his vision, which is why, I think, the plain people of his time adored him.

Still the impenetrability of his nature, the elusiveness of his style, rendered him a hard man to figure out, both when he was alive and after his death. Thus the most steadily acute observer of American public affairs in this century—Walter Lippmann—made his famous observation in 1932 that Roosevelt was "a pleasant man who, without any important qualifications for the office, would very much like to be President." People constantly got him wrong, then and later; and in the more than quarter century since his death he has continued to defy historians and biographers. In Joseph Lash's beautiful book *Eleanor and Franklin* Mrs. Roosevelt is a finely and fully realized character, but Franklin Roosevelt remains an enigmatic and perplexing presence.

The problem of FDR's place in history is compounded by the turbulence of his time and ours—and especially by the changing shapes the rush of his years has given to the problems with which he dealt. Thus for a long time historians condemned Roosevelt's First New Deal, with its concentration on structure and planning, as a bad turn, a wrong road, a gravely mistaken diversion of energy and administration, happily replaced after 1935 by a new concentration on compensatory fiscal policy and on the revival of the market through antitrust action. This judgment prevailed so long as Keynesianism appeared to contain the solution to our economic dilemmas. But, as we have come to understand that fiscal policy by itself cannot restrain inflation in an economy controlled by the concentration of market power in large corporations and unions, we will come, I believe, to detect new virtues in the experimentation of 1933 and 1934. I wrote thirteen years ago in *The Coming of the New Deal* that

the economic philosophy of NRA was by no means so mistaken as its conventional critics have assumed. . . . In accepting the logic of the administered market, NRA accepted the responsibility for acting directly on the relationships of prices, wages and profits. It rejected the supposition that general principles could solve specific relationships in an equitable or productive way. It presumed instead that the solution of these problems—and, beyond this, the use and allocation of resources through the economy—required a considerable integration of public and private planning, in which business, labor and consumers as well as government should play a part. While its institutions were too sketchy and improvised, too distorted by special interest and too confused by melodrama, to come near realizing its objective, NRA still operated in terms of a fairly realistic picture of the modern market.

Now, in the current age of Phase I and Phase II, where in vital sectors industry and labor to a considerable degree set their own prices and wages, we are coming to see, I think, that we cannot dodge the challenge of structure and planning that Roosevelt tried to explore nearly forty years ago.

Let me suggest another example—this time from foreign policy—to show again how our contemporary perceptions reshape our judgment of the past. For a long time it was fashionable to condemn as hopeless naiveté Roosevelt's determination to deal personally with Stalin during the Second World War; it was folly, we were told, for FDR to suppose that he could charm or beguile Stalin into postwar cooperation. And certainly there can be no doubt that Stalin, seeing the world through the lenses of Marxism-Leninism, had a deeply ingrained belief that the mere existence of a capitalist United States was, by definition, a deadly threat to the security of the Soviet Union. Nor can there be any doubt either that Roosevelt's indifference to and ignorance of Marxist-Leninist ideology hardly helped him around the conference tables of Teheran and Yalta.

Still Stalin was by no means a helpless prisoner of that ideology. He saw himself, as Averell Harriman has reminded us, less as the disciple of Marx and Lenin than as their fellow prophet. As the infallible expositor, he could interpret the faith to justify anything he wanted to do at any given moment. In retrospect, I think it will increasingly appear that Roosevelt's determination to deal personally with him was an expression of astute political insight. Roosevelt intuitively understood that Stalin was the best means then available to the West to amend Leninist ideology and to deflect the thrust of Soviet totalitarianism—that Stalin was, so to speak, the only force in 1945 capable of overcoming Stalinism. The best evidence is that Roosevelt retained a certain capacity to influence Stalin to the end; Yalta was an indication of that. It is in this way that the death of Roosevelt was crucial in the rise of the Cold War—not in the vulgar sense that his policy was then reversed by his successor, which did not happen, but in the sense that no other American could hope to have the restraining impact on Stalin that, for a while, Roosevelt might have had.

As we perceive the present differently, so we perceive the past differently: hence the inconstancy of history. And the problem is further compounded by the variety of grounds for our present perceptions; above all, by the variety of political grounds. Here an examination of Roosevelt's reputation becomes a rich study in irony. In his own time conservatives denounced him as a radical, a Socialist, a revolutionary, an enemy of the American way of life, a President bent on desecrating the verities and destroying the system. Today the zealots of New Left history attack him on opposite grounds. They see him as a compromiser, a cunning opportunist who, behind radical rhetoric, sought to protect and reestablish the profit system, the most clever and effective of the champions of corporate capitalism. Foreign policy provides equivalent ironies. For the first decade after Roosevelt's death, he was the man who appeased Stalin, sold Eastern Europe and China down the river into slavery and connived at Communist conspiracy within the United States. Today, under the New Left revelation, he becomes the father of American imperialism, the leader who, beneath the guise of universalist slogans, sought only to make the world safe for penetration and domination by American trade and American capital, the man who, Professor Chomsky tells us, forced war on the beleaguered Japanese and who, Professor William

Appleman Williams assures us, opposed Nazism primarily because Hitler threatened to obstruct the establishment through the world of American economic hegemony. It is an additional irony that, in so many respects, the New Left is thus coming to occupy the positions of the Old Right.

Because Roosevelt himself was so baffling a man and because the problems of his age change as our perspectives on them change, one may expect the historical controversy to continue unabated for a long time into the future. It is hard even to conclude whether Roosevelt's major success lay in the field of domestic or of foreign policy. One historian, Robert A. Divine, has recently written, "Roosevelt's claim to greatness must rest on his achievements in domestic affairs. His conduct of foreign policy never equaled his mastery of American politics and his ability to guide the nation through the perils of depression and war." Yet others would salute his prescience in foreign affairs and add that there were still 8 million Americans—one sixth of the labor force—unemployed in 1940; that Roosevelt himself, for all the concessions he made on humanitarian grounds to the need for public spending, probably remained to the end a budget-balancer at heart; and that ominous trends in our policy—the centralization and bureaucratization of government, the militarization of foreign policy, the rise of the secrecy system, the emergence of the FBI as a political force—all received great impetus in the Roosevelt years.

A longer view would perhaps seek to locate Roosevelt in the great, rushing, roaring stream of change generated in the modern world by scientific and technological innovation. Henry Adams was the first American historian to call attention to the increasing acceleration of history—an acceleration that with mounting force disrupts our ideas, our values, our institutions and the very stability of our lives. Riding the rapids of change is not the easiest of tasks. Holding to the past is no solution; nor has anyone yet produced a dependable chart of the future. Dogma is a drag in a world of flux, contingency and unpredictability. What is required is imagination, flexibility, a capacity for innovation, a sense of adventure, an ability to inspire others with confidence and a sense of purpose—this and a vision, not ideologized or rigid, but capacious, sensitive and strong, of the kind of nation and the kind of world toward which we aspire. When a very young man, Winston Churchill once wrote to an American politician, "The duty of governments is to be first of all practical. I am for makeshifts and expediency. I would like to make the people who live on this world at the same time as I do better fed and happier generally. If incidentally I benefit posterity—so much the better—but I would not sacrifice my own generation to a principle—however high, or a truth, however great." This passionate sense that concrete humanity is all was doubtless one of the things that bound Roosevelt and Churchill together in their marvelous partnership.

Coming to the presidency when an industrial society, choked on its own mechanisms, seemed to be losing its capacity to function, Roosevelt fiddled with the machinery, succored the victims and casualties and got the contraption started again. Confronted by a world menaced by an armed fanaticism determined to murder or subjugate the rest of mankind, Roosevelt understood rather early, I think, the size of the threat; with patience and cajolery he slowly persuaded his fellow citizens that the threat was real; and he led his country to victory in the greatest war of history. In doing these things, he reinvigorated popular faith in the efficacy of democratic government and in the continuing vitality of his nation's best ideals. If Theodore Roosevelt and Woodrow Wilson represented the first stage in the national encounter with the velocity of history and the anguish of the twentieth century, Franklin Roosevelt, with immense *brio*, force and courage, carried us into the next stage, learning and teaching through error as well as through success. To say that he did not solve the problems he faced hardly diminishes the astonishing power of his achievement. "Great men," wrote Emerson, "exist that there may be greater men."

Let new generations take up where Franklin Roosevelt left off—and try to do better.

He was unquestionably a great President—along with Lincoln and Washington, the greatest in our history—great in his instinct for problems and possibilities, in his strength of leadership and purpose and in his capacity to restore the confidence of the people in themselves. He was also a flawed President, even though, as we have seen, one man's flaw may be the next man's virtue. "Some people," wrote La Rochefoucauld, "resemble ballads, which are only sung for a certain time." Roosevelt, I have no doubt, will be sung throughout the life of our nation—most of all, perhaps, because he lived in the spirit about which Emerson wrote:

If there is any period one would desire to be born in—is it not the era of revolution when the old and the new stand side by side and admit of being compared; when all the energies of man are searched by fear and hope; when the historic glories of the old can be compensated by the rich possibilities of the new era? This time like all times is a very good one if one but knows what to do with it.

More than any of his contemporaries, Roosevelt knew what to do with his time.

CONTEMPORARY MOODS: SACRED AND PROFANE

THE PRAYER AMENDMENT [1]

JAMES G. HARRIS [2]

The question concerning prayer in the public schools has agitated many sincere churchgoers since the Supreme Court (*Engel v. Vitale,* 370, U.S. 421, 1962) and other courts ruled that Bible reading and organized prayers in public schools are a violation of the First and Fourteenth Amendments to the Constitution. After failing to devise a nondenominational prayer acceptable to the courts, the prayer advocates, originally led by Senator Everett Dirksen, proposed the passage of a Constitutional amendment to legalize prayer in the public schools.

More recently, under the leadership of Mrs. Ben Ruhlin, "a little housewife from Cuyahoga Falls," Ohio, the prayer forces organized the Prayer Campaign Committee, a widely supported grassroots lobby. Working through civic and religious groups, this lobby exerted its influence across the country, challenging politicians who refused to support the amendment and apparently bringing defeat to some congressmen who resisted. Mrs. Ruhlin recently produced a petition of 100,000 signatures to bring pressure on wavering legislators. Representative Chalmers Wylie (Republican, Ohio) carried the fight to the House. In a highly unusual occurrence, he was able to secure 218 signatures of fellow representatives to force the proposed amendment out of the Judiciary Committee, over the Committee's vigorous objections. Public opinion polls heavily favored the amendment, but leading legal authorities, churchmen, and major religious organizations opposed it.

Debates in the House of Representatives seldom stir much interest or lead to very vigorous speaking, in part because of the size of the body and the strict limitations on the time allotted to each representative. But the debate over the prayer amendment

[1] Delivered at the University Baptist Church, Fort Worth, Texas, October 3, 1971. Quoted by permission.

[2] For biographical note, see Appendix.

on November 8, 1971, produced good attendance and earnest speaking as a number of representatives stood up for what they believed. The amendment stated:

> Nothing contained in this Constitution shall abridge the right of persons lawfully assembled, in any public building which is supported in whole or in part through expenditure of public funds, to participate in nondenominational prayer.

During the debate Representative G. V. Montgomery (Democrat, Mississippi) frankly warned his colleagues what opposition to the amendment might mean:

> Let us lay our cards on the table. A vote for the proposed constitutional amendment is going to be a lot easier to explain back home than a vote against it. I know that if I vote against the resolution today, my opponent next year will make me do a lot of explaining.

Representative Wylie put the case for the affirmative well when he said:

> We have an opportunity right now, in this the people's House, to allow the people to speak—to debate this issue in the legislative halls of the fifty states. This is the kind of safety valve provided for in the Constitution and, because of the confusion and frustration, such a debate could be meaningful.
>
> We have a motto above our clock—"In God We Trust." It is time we returned to an unapologetic recognition of that basic principle in the public schools of our nation. (*Congressional Record*, November 8, 1971 page H 10644)

Taking the other side of the question, the Rev. James G. Harris of the University Baptist Church of Fort Worth made the prayer amendment the subject of his sermon on Sunday, October 31, 1971. He gave a clear presentation of the issues involved and the reasons for his opposition to the amendment in the speech reprinted below.

In terms of homiletical structure the speech falls under the classification of a topical sermon, meaning that it is developed from an idea rather than a scriptural passage. The reader will note that the sermon contains no citation from biblical authority; instead it is built around logical premises shared by the listeners. To persons who favor restricting the minister to scriptural subjects the sermon will be disturbing, but it will please those who encourage the clergy to play active roles in contemporary affairs. Avoiding generalities and platitudes, jargon and clichés, the sermon is a straightforward, well-organized presentation of a significant issue.

On November 8, 1971, the House of Representatives rejected the proposed constitutional amendment that would have permitted "voluntary" prayers in public schools.

On November 8, just one week from tomorrow, House Joint Resolution 191 will be introduced on the floor of Congress. It shall be subject to a vote without passing through the Judiciary Committee, where hearings could have cleared the air and where opponents to this bill would have had a chance to be heard in reasons for their vigorous opposition.

In 1964, three months were spent in hearings when a so-called prayer amendment, the Becker Amendment, was proposed. As a result of these hearings, the overwhelming evidence presented to the Committee was so convincing that the effort was abandoned. At that time, to avoid such a hearing, the so-called prayer lobbyists sought to get the necessary 218 signatures of congressmen that would have made it possible to bypass the Judiciary Committee and eliminate the hearings that are so necessary for a thorough study of a bill. Only 170 signatures could be obtained in 1964.

The champions of freedom won a great victory and we relaxed. But the other side did not relax. For seven years they have lobbied and worked. After these intervening years, a discharge petition was signed a few days ago by the required 218 congressmen, and within a matter of days this bill will be presented on the floor of the House. We who are concerned and alarmed have little time to turn the tide around. I bring this message to inform you of what I believe is a grave peril to our liberty and to share with you my own convictions.

In a press conference in Washington earlier this month, Congressman James Corman of California, an opponent of the bill, predicted that it would be defeated in the House. Congressman Emanuel Celler, Chairman of the Judiciary Committee and long-time foe of this amendment, sharply turned to Dr. Carl E. Bates, president of the Southern Baptist Convention, and said, "It will not be defeated unless religious groups do more to inform their people about the principles involved in this." This is my purpose for taking this valuable time to preach on this political and religious issue.

The resolution reads as follows:

Nothing contained in this Constitution shall abridge the right of persons lawfully assembled in any public building which is supported in whole or in part through the expenditure of public funds, to participate in nondenominational prayer.

If this effort succeeds, then the Bill of Rights of the Constitution will be amended for the first time in history. The Fort Worth *Star Telegram,* in an editorial in 1964, wrote: "The First Amendment has permitted religious freedom to thrive in the United States as in no other country past or present." The editorial continued, "It would take a very good amendment indeed to improve on that record."

And this proposed amendment is not a good one. It would add nothing to the liberties we already enjoy. I believe it would actually weaken the Constitution that for nearly two hundred years has given us such freedom.

The First Amendment to the Constitution says, "Congress shall make no law respecting an establishment of religion, or prohibiting the free exercise thereof."

This so-called prayer amendment grows out of the basic misunderstanding and misinterpretation of decisions made by the Supreme Court in 1962 and 1963.

In 1962, the Court ruled against the compulsory reciting of a prayer composed by the State, on the part of the children in our public schools. The Court did not rule against prayer. They did not make God illegal. They ruled against agents of the state writing a prayer and prescribing that it should be read in a daily ritual in every public school in the state. There are no constitutional restrictions against voluntary prayer in the schools. What the court was saying was, "No government agent, no school board, no school superintendent, no schoolteacher has a right to tell a school child *when* to pray! *where* to pray! *what* to pray!" Do you not agree with that principle?

The decision in 1963 decreed that no government agent could *require* Bible reading in the public schools. The Court said further that no public authority could *require* the recitation of the Lord's Prayer in public schools. The Constitution says Congress has no right to prohibit the *free* exercise of religion, and the Court upheld that proclamation. Compulsory prayer is not the *free* exercise of religion. Required Bible reading is not the *free* exercise of religion. The recitation of the Christian prayer, called the Lord's Prayer, by mandate by the state is not *free* exercise of religion.

Representative Fred Schwengel, a Baptist Congressman, addressed a Baptist group. He said, "We ought to be *applauding* the Supreme Court in these cases. We ought to hang our heads in shame that an atheist, Mrs. Madalyn Murray O'Hare, took this to the Supreme Court, when we Baptists should have."

We sympathize with the zealous desire of many misguided people who misunderstand the decisions of the Supreme Court. They sincerely believe that they are fighting to preserve the right of all persons to pray. They believe that this amendment will restore prayer to its proper place and will reintroduce God to our public life. But if this amendment becomes a part of our Constitution, I prophesy that they shall have actually weakened the practice of prayer, which they have sought to strengthen. Today we have a constitutional right to pray a nondenominational or a denominational prayer in public buildings or private buildings. This amendment would specifically define the content of my prayers. When I pray before a football game in the stadium of the University of Texas or in the halls of Congress before a daily session of the House of Representatives, I must pray a nondenominational prayer. I have prayed the invocation in football stadiums of public schools. In 1958, I delivered the daily prayer in the hall of Congress. In each instance, I prayed a *Christian* prayer, without apology or shame or condemnation. If this amendment passes, in the future I would be required to pray an innocuous, unoffending, nebulous, neutral petition that neither God nor man would listen to. I would have to submit it in advance to a government authority to determine if it was a nondenominational prayer, whatever that means. I could still preach a Christian sermon at a high school baccalaureate service, but I would have to present in advance the text of my prayer, so that all concerned would be assured that it was nondenominational.

If I understand my Bible, the prayer of a Christian is a prayer in Jesus' name. I respect the prayer of my Jewish friend, of the Moslem, the Hindu, or the Buddhist. I respect their right to pray their prayer when they stand in a public meeting. I must reserve that same right.

What is a nondenominational prayer? Who determines if it is nondenominational? The state—through its officials and its courts! This would make the government a judge of theology and an administrator of religious practice. Would this increase our freedom, our constitutional right to the free exercise of our religion?

Who is capable of composing a nondenominational prayer? Who is capable of judging its content? After the 1964 struggle, Congressman Celler said, "Our Committee was unable to devise language which it could recommend to the House that would not do violence to religious freedom now guaranteed by the First Amendment." There is no language that man can devise that would not weaken what our founding fathers wrote.

I deeply sympathize with the position of our congressmen. To vote against this amendment is to threaten their political survival. A United States Senator was defeated in Texas last year partly because of the accusation of his opponent that he was "against prayer," because he courageously opposed the prayer amendment in 1964. In the same way, fanatical people will accuse your congressman of being "against God" if he opposes this amendment. These men need our assurance that we shall stand by them if they are exploited and abused because of their stand for freedom. Let us convince them that there are more of us who will commend them than there are of those who would condemn them. They need to hear from us.

There is much less justification today for this effort to amend the Constitution than there was during the hysteria of 1964. The Court had just handed down two decisions that looked like they were headed toward total secularization. The threat of the Becker Amendment in 1964 could have caused our high court to reverse its direction at the time. Not a single decision has been declared in these eight ensuing years that would threaten the freedom of voluntary prayer in public assemblies. Even if there had been a need for an amendment in 1964, although I deny that there was, there is certainly no need for it today.

The trend of the present Supreme Court is actually in the opposite direction. President Nixon has appointed four strict constructionists to the Court. Two of these are seated on the bench and the other two are now under consideration for approval by the Senate. How tragic that in these days when there is less threat than ever to the free exercise of prayer in public life, we should consider tampering with this First Amendment that has stood for two hundred years.

The Fort Worth *Star Telegram* recently wrote in an editorial, "Such an amendment would open the doors for governmental intrusion into the religious affairs of the people." We would be saying, "Congress shall not interfere with the free exercise of religion except in the area of prayer in public assembly, where the Government will dictate the kind of prayer and the content of the prayer that is delivered." After one exception has been attached to the First Amendment, what is to prevent other exceptions to the free exercise of religion in future years? Let us oppose *any* exception and preserve the Bill of Rights as it is.

The Southern Baptist Convention adopted unanimously a resolution last June opposing this amendment. Are we against prayer? The Baptist General Convention of Texas adopted without dissent a resolution last week opposing this Amendment. Are we atheistic? The National Council of Churches, the United Methodist Church, the Presbyterians, the Lutherans have taken their stand against this bill. The only Catholic priest in Congress is fighting against its passage. I do not know a Baptist state editor who has not editorialized against it. I do not know a seminary professor who supports it. Doesn't all of this tell us something?

Prayer is intensely personal, a very denominational exercise. The Constitution protects our right to keep it so. We need to heed the words of Kierkegaard, "There is that which is more contrary to Christianity . . . than any heresy, any schism . . . and that is to *play* Christianity."

FREAKS FOR JESUS' SAKE [3]

EDWARD L. R. ELSON [4]

Change is the order of the day. It is coming to government, business, politics, education, and very much to religion, particularly among youth. In addition to experimentation with drugs, new morality, and group living, youth groups are questioning organized religion and searching for new avenues to religious and mystical experiences. The popular rock opera *Jesus Christ Superstar,* which presents Jesus as human, not divine, is a barometer of youthful moods and sentiments. Some seek satisfaction in Oriental mysticism: Vedanta, a variety of Hinduism; Yoga, an Indian faith; Bahai, an offshoot of Islam; and the Japanese faith "Strangers at the Door." On city streets and campuses have appeared followers of the Hindu deity Krishna, in saffron robes, with shaved heads and painted faces, chanting: "Hare Krishna, Hare Krishna, Krishna Krishna, Hare Hare." Others have participated in more conventional groups, such as Fellowship of Christian Athletes and the Campus Crusade for Christ. Increasing numbers have affiliated with the Roman Catholic Pentecostals, the Jesus People (Jesus Freaks), and the Children of God. The Jesus movement has even spread to US Army camps in Europe. (Officers report that converts are better soldiers.)

Dr. Elton Trueblood, a widely respected Quaker teacher, writer, and philosopher of Earlham College, interprets that Jesus People as follows:

> The new people calling themselves the "Jesus People" and termed by their detractors "Jesus Freaks" have sprung up with apparent spontaneity in many different parts of our country in the last few months. Characteristically, the adherents of the new movement are relatively young people who have been part of the drug culture against which they

[3] Delivered at the National Presbyterian Church, Washington, D.C., June 27, 1971. Quoted by permission.

[4] For biographical note, see Appendix.

have revolted after they have seen that drugs are unable to meet any fundamental human needs. In a mood of desperation they have turned to Jesus as a viable alternative to their former despair and disillusionment. In their commitment to Jesus, many seem to have discovered a new way of ordering their emotions as well as liberation from the bondage of both compulsive drug use and obsession with sex.

The new life in which these people now rejoice is one of almost continuous hilarity. They shout and sing and call out to anyone who will listen, "Jesus loves you." As is not very surprising, they often retain some of the external marks of their former way of life, including long hair and strict conformity in dress. While adopting a new gospel, they retain the appearance and many of the manners of hippies. This paradox is responsible for much of the attention accorded them by the news media. They are bound to make news in a way which neither the conventional hippie nor the conventional Christian make it. (*Yokefellows International,* December 1971.)

These movements, stirred by motivations outside organized religion, greatly distress many sincere and devout persons. For example, some parents assert that the Children of God have kidnaped, hypnotized, or drugged their children. The communal living, the strange ceremonies, the prayer vigils, the taking of new names, the giving up of worldly possessions—these are interpreted by many as signs of a sinister influence.

Dr. Edward L. R. Elson, prominent Presbyterian clergyman and chaplain of the United States Senate, was well aware that members of his distinguished congregation at the National Presbyterian Church in Washington, D. C., were disturbed by those popularly labeled as Jesus Freaks; consequently on June 27, 1971, he devoted his sermon to the subject.

The sermon is a topical one developed around a current problem instead of a passage from the Scriptures. The sermon suggests that the speaker had carefully researched his subject, for he presented a well-conceived interpretation of the Jesus People. He makes a plea for understanding and compassion. Perhaps his reference to Paul as a Jesus Freak may have jolted some of his more conservative or fundamentalist listeners, but he did find a comparison to evoke thought and meditation. The language is simple, appropriate, and effective—avoiding what so often seems artificial and overwrought in the pulpit.

> No one should think that I am a fool. But if you do, at
> least accept me as a fool. . . . But if anyone dares to boast
> of something—I am talking like a fool—I will be just as
> daring.
> —II Corinthians 11:16, 21 (Today's English Version)

I hold in my hands and display to you a copy of one of
the most interesting newspapers I have read in many years.
Reflected at the top is the dome of the Capitol across which
is superimposed the title of the paper *The Liberator,* with
the symbol of a forefinger of the right hand pointing heaven-
ward and beside which is a Latin cross. The full title of this
paper is *Jesus Christ Is "The Liberator,"* published by the
Jesus People. The headline of this issue on its front page is
"Jesus People: Here To Stay!"

The leading editorial is written by William Willoughby,
staff writer for the Washington *Star,* who last night spoke to
the young married couples club of our church, the Tuggs, at
their monthly meeting, which was held on the beach.

Some people are writing, as in the current issue of *Time*
magazine, about the Jesus Revolution. Others devote many
paragraphs to the Jesus Freaks. The July issue of *Harper's*
carried an article by Sara Davidson entitled "The Rush for
Instant Salvation." The most recent book by the Quaker
writer Elton Trueblood has the title *The Future of the
Christian.*

More than a year ago, on the campus of Asbury College
in Kentucky there broke out a spontaneous spiritual awaken-
ing which continued without interruption for many weeks.
There had been no preparation for it, no evangelist sum-
moned people to repent and confess Christ. What happened
was that first one college student after another, prompted by
some unexplained inner urge, stood up before groups of students ranging from little clusters to vast crowds, and confessed that they had been delivered from the burden of sin
and defeat and had found joy and power through the living
Christ. Although the college life continued, prayer and witnessing was uninterrupted. From that center students on

weekends traveled to colleges all over America where they gave personal witness to the new-found reality of the living Christ in several hundred colleges. Other groups of students caught the spirit. The movement has infected the whole of American academic life in a manner not unlike that which happened in earlier American history in the days of Jonathan Edwards, Charles G. Finney, and Dwight L. Moody, as well as resembling in some manner that which took place in eighteenth century England under the leadership of two brothers in the Anglican ministry, John and Charles Wesley. There has been no explanation except in the supernatural power of the Holy Spirit.

Look at other bits of the current scene. Some years ago, guided by Dr. Louis H. Evans, Sr., former pastor of the Hollywood First Presbyterian Church, there came into being what is now a tremendous movement called the Fellowship of Christian Athletes. The members of this association are athletes in high school, in college, and in professional football, basketball, and baseball who are unashamedly out-and-out Christians. They hold conferences, institutes, and summer camps now attended by thousands of young athletes. Although some of the leaders have now given up their professional careers as athletes, completed their seminary education, and give full-time leadership to the movement, the genius of this group is that it is a fellowship of young Christian athletes who testify to a life transformed, made vital and meaningful in day-by-day living. Some years ago they asked me to write the story of the influence of my high school football coach upon my Christian life and my decision to enter the ministry. They made it a front-cover story.

On college and university campuses there is also a movement called Inter-Varsity Christian Fellowship which, while never pretending to substitute for or compete with the organized denominational representation on the campus, nevertheless seems to have the greatest vitality for influencing the personal lives of university students of any movement on American campuses.

Time magazine pointed out that:

few groups have had more impact than has one man, Assemblies of God minister David Wilkerson, whose growing movement began with a single incident: his dramatic conversion of Brooklyn teenage gang lord Nicky Cruz in 1958. Cruz . . . is now an evangelist. Wilkerson's evangelical and antidrug organization Teen Challenge has fifty-three centers. His book about Cruz' conversion, *The Cross and the Switchblade,* has sold six million copies. The movie version starring Pat Boone as Wilkerson will be released nationwide, July 1st.

Last year at the annual meeting of the Religious Heritage of America we became better acquainted with this phenomenal movement by the presence in our city of both Wilkerson and Pat Boone. Among other influences of the Teen Challenge group and Wilkerson is the pentecostal flavor which helped launch the Roman Catholic pentecostal movement which is an extraordinary feature of the lives of many Roman Catholics today.

How are we who belong to the principal religious denominations of Christendom, in the Catholic and Reformed traditions, to evaluate these movements and forces and relate them to the Church today?

Mr. Willoughby opens his editorial with these words:

I am 100 percent convinced that these must be the most exciting days in the world's history—more specifically, the history of the Church of Jesus Christ. It is becoming increasingly evident that a revival of spiritual life that focuses on the power of the Holy Spirit and the glorification of Christ is taking place—a revival such as not even the first-century Christians witnessed.

This is a very bold assessment by one who is perhaps the best student of the movements in our country.

Willoughby goes on to say that he believes this powerful movement is anything but a fad and that it is something which cannot be stopped. The Jesus Freaks are using four-letter words—words like *love* and *pray*. They are making forays into the topless and bottomless joints in San Francisco and giving an unmistakable witness that such things are not right. There they are, looking a good bit like hippies, some are converted Maoists or Black Panthers or Free Speech Radicals, now suddenly possessed of a zeal of pleasing God.

What are these people doing?

It is a startling development [says *Time*], for a generation that has constantly been accused of tripping out or copping out with sex, drugs, and violence, now embracing the most persistent symbol of purity, selflessness, and brotherly love in the history of Western man, aflame with a pentecostal passion for sharing their new vision with others. Fresh-faced, wide-eyed young girls and earnest young men badger businessmen and shoppers on Hollywood Boulevard, or near the Lincoln Memorial, in Dallas, Detroit, Wichita, or San Francisco, witnessing for Christ with reckless exhortations.

Nearly twenty-five years ago this congregation through the Sunday Evening Club opened in the basement of our old church at Connecticut Avenue and N Street the first church-sponsored coffeehouse in Washington. Now there are many of them, such as the Coffee House on Columbia Road, sponsored by the Church of Our Savior, the King's Inn in Alexandria, others in Georgetown, the Dupont Circle area, and on Capitol Hill. As one person put it, these " 'Christian houses' are multiplying like loaves and fishes for youngsters hungry for homes, many reaching out to the troubled with round-the-clock telephone hot lines."

Almost all of them are reading the Bible and discussing it. Founder Bill Bright of the Campus Crusade for Christ says, "Our target date for saturating the United States with the gospel of Jesus Christ is 1976—and the world by 1980." This is reminiscent of the haystack prayer meeting at a New England university in another age which launched the Student volunteer movement with its motto, "The Evangelization of the World in This Generation." For some there is the fascination for Jesus out of hero-worship of a fellow rebel, the first great martyr to the cause of peace and brotherhood. But this is not the attitude of the vast majority toward Jesus. The one mark which clearly identifies them is their total belief in an awesome, supernatural Jesus Christ, not just a marvelous man who lived two thousand years ago but a living God who is both Savior and Judge, the Ruler of their destinies. Their lives revolve around the necessity for an intense personal relationship with Jesus and the belief that such a relationship should condition every human life. They act as if divine intervention guides their every movement and can be counted upon to solve every problem. Many are redeemed from personal rebellion against all of society or from drug addiction and now subscribe strictly to the Ten Commandments rather than the "new morality" and, like earlier Christians, are sometimes intolerant of failures among new converts.

Everywhere there is testimony to a new life, a new purpose, and a tremendous revolution. Maureen Orth, in a supplement to the book *Whole Earth Catalog* writes: "The first thing I realized is how different it is to go to high school today. Acid trips in the seventh grade, sex in the eighth, the Vietnam war a daily serial on TV since you were nine. Parents and school worse than irrelevant—meaningless. No wonder Jesus is making a great comeback!"

The truth is that the death of authority brought the curse of uncertainty.

"The freedom from work, from restraint, from accountability, wondrous in its inception, became banal and counterfeit. Without rules there was no way to say no, and worse, no way to say yes," wrote Thomas Farber in his little book entitled *Tales for the Son of My Unborn Child*. Richard Hoag believes that many of his youthful converts see Jesus as a marvelous father figure: "The kids are searching for authority, love, and understanding, ingredients missing at home. Jesus is what their fathers aren't." One pastor says, "I am amazed at how many people I have counseled who have never heard their father say 'I love you.' "

The movement at present, we must conclude, is not against established religion but rather apart from it. The

Rev. Robert E. Terwilliger of New York City's Trinity Institute says, "There is a revival of religion everywhere except in the Church." We Christians who love the Church must now show our love to all persons who call Christ Lord, whether they follow our patterns of expression or appear to be by our standards bizarre or eccentric. We must be careful lest too much we love the Church just as it is and do not love Christ sufficiently to allow the Holy Spirit to make us and the Church become what it ought to be in our age.

The Church, we must repeat over and over again, is not an institution, much less a building. The Church has been institutionalized in order to promote the gospel of redeeming love and it has buildings in order to shelter its activities and provide centers from which its influence might radiate to the whole world. These institutions and these visible symbols have served the Church well and can continue to do so. But the Church and all of us in it must be open to the leadership of the Holy Spirit, be prepared for surprises, and always to welcome to our affection and our community life all those who truly follow Jesus Christ even though they do it in their way rather than in our way. When some of the young people among the Jesus Freaks have been asked which church they belong to, they have replied, "We are the Church." Although they may not have formulated the profounder statements of Christian theology which we are heir to through the great historic Confession and Creeds of the Church, these "new Christians" bear a strange resemblance to the first-century Christians who turned the world upside down. By every measurement we have today the greatest Christian evangelist, missionary and theologian the world has ever known would be described as a Jesus Freak.

St. Paul was called a fool and he used the word *fool* to describe himself.

In the first place, Paul must have been a Jesus Freak in his personal appearance. Tradition says he was not a prepossessing personality. He was small of stature, bald-headed, and bow-legged. He had some physical malady which he called his "thorn in the flesh," which tormented him all his life. When he spoke his words came not through a massive, majestic, male personality whose physical appearance "wowed" his hearers. His words came through a wizened, weak little frame of a Jesus Freak.

Paul was an intellectual freak. He is often regarded as the greatest intellect of his time, but judged by the intellectual outlook of his age he was a freak. He was learned in the Scriptures, the complicated legalism of Judaism, its history, its philosophy, its practices. He was well educated in Hellenistic or Greek thought, he was a Roman citizen and knew full well all that Roman life, law, and power meant. And he was one of the most traveled men of his age. Yet it was not his knowledge of all these forces which gave him power. His sermon on Mars Hill fell flat while he drew upon these sources of his intellect. He was a religious expert in all these fields, but it was through the "foolishness of preaching" what came to be called the Gospel that his power came through.

His message was that this Jesus of Nazareth who taught, healed, and went about in the body of a man, like the rest of us, made known in that single life the greatest truths and the most vivid reality we can have about God. This Jesus of Nazareth, who was rejected by His own people, arrested, tried, and put to death as a criminal, nevertheless was not destroyed by death but made Himself known to His followers after arising from the grave. This conquering man's last enemy, death, was the certification that He was in fact the Son of God whom God sent to free men from sin and destruction. This same Jesus of Nazareth on Easter morning arose from the tomb to become the Living Christ of the ages—that He was even now present, alive, vivid, and would bring to fulfillment any human being who in true repentance and faith came to Him.

In our text for today Paul said, as he wrote his second letter to the Corinthians, "No one should think that I am a fool. But if you do, at least accept me as a fool. . . . But if anyone dares to boast of something—I am talking like a fool —I will be just as daring." Wouldn't this be a good clue for us today?

On the scene today I see two great movements, both fundamentalist in their character and pretensions. The one is the Jesus Freaks, with their Bible study, prayer, praise, and radically changed personalities reaching people with a gospel that can only be called supernatural. They have a hard time being patient or even considering as credible those Christians who have not had their kind of experience. There is another group of Jesus Freaks. They are the activists who tend to minimize instant personal conversion but want instant conversion of society—the immediate transformation of cities, elimination of poverty, absolute justice and banishment of war. They tend to think their methods and their program are sacrosanct and the only divinely approved way of achieving the objectives. Some of them absolutize church resolutions, lift them to the level of theological dogma and make heretics of all those who differ with them.

Neither the Jesus Freaks for instant personal conversion nor the Jesus Freaks for instant sociological conversion have the whole gospel. There must be a synthesis of the two. The synthesis comes not in institutions, much less by pronouncements, but in persons. And the Church must be big enough in its love and inclusive enough in its fellowship to help each group find the other. The call to us today is to be unafraid of the destructive powers of evil in our world and to welcome the constructive powers of God's Holy Spirit which are ready to renew and empower the Church. The New Testament calls Christ the "dynamite" of God. Let us close with words which ring out from the last book of the Bible, "Even so come, Lord Jesus."

A LEARNING SOCIETY

THE INSTITUTIONAL ILLUSION [1]

ROBERT M. HUTCHINS [2]

Some persons have called Robert M. Hutchins, Jr., "a fanatical liberal," while others see him as "ominously medieval." First as president and chancellor of the University of Chicago (1929-1951) and more recently as chairman and chief executive officer of the Fund for the Republic (since 1954), he has called for serious reform in education and in the university. He has opposed specialized and technical training in higher education, rigid departmentalization, and the present university structure (particularly the so-called multiversity). He has argued for emphasis upon the liberal arts and the extension of learning beyond the campus. On one occasion he succinctly declared:

> Ideal education is the one that develops intellectual power. . . . The ideal education is not an *ad hoc* education, not an education directed to immediate needs; it is not a specialized education, or a preprofessional education; it is not a utilitarian education. It is an education calculated to develop the mind (from *A Conversation on Education,* 1963).

Appropriately, the speech that follows was delivered in Chicago on April 3, 1971, twenty years after Hutchins left the University of Chicago, at a convocation of members of the Center for the Study of Democratic Institutions, a branch arm of the Fund for the Republic, meeting at the Palmer House. He epitomizes his thinking as follows: "We can have a learning society. Its object would be to raise every man and woman and every community to the highest cultural level attainable."

The speech is filled with bold assertions supported by vivid examples from a lifetime of thinking, study, discussion, and experience. Hutchins' opinions stir vigorous objections from those who hold to what he calls "the institutional illusion." Some readers may

---

[1] Delivered at a symposium entitled "Toward a Learning Society," Palmer House, Chicago, Illinois, April 3, 1971. In a slightly revised form, printed in *Center Magazine* IV (July/August 1971), 42-7. Quoted by permission.

[2] For biographical note, see Appendix.

think that this presentation is only a restatement of what Hutchins has said before. If such criticism has any validity, then the answer may be that what Hutchins says needs to be said again. (For another speech, see "The University and the Multiversity," *New Republic,* April 1, 1967.)

What A. Craig Baird wrote in the introduction to the last Hutchins speech published in REPRESENTATIVE AMERICAN SPEECHES: 1951-1952 is probably still true:

> Speech students rate Hutchins as one of the four or five best speakers among educational leaders. His voice is resonant, well controlled, persuasive. His bearing is impressive and dominant. He is fluent and especially effective in extempore utterance. Wherever he has spoken he has "stirred up" his audience. On the platform he is at his best when answering challenging questions from the floor.

Although he now accepts fewer invitations than in former days, Hutchins is still one of the most provocative and effective academic speakers of our time.

I have journeyed from my jasmine-scented bower in Santa Barbara first because I wanted to sit once more at the feet of my mentors and coconspirators George Shuster and Champ Ward, and second because I wanted to take part again in the argument about education that went on in the University and the community of Chicago all the time I lived here and that I have no doubt continues to this day.

We didn't talk much about the prospects for a learning society in those remote times. We were having enough trouble trying to make sense of what we were doing already. And we couldn't really imagine a learning society. We knew about technology and knew that technological change would make idiots of those who thought people should be trained to acquire technical skill. We knew that because John Dewey had told us so when he was a member of the Chicago community in 1897. We saw that the aim of education must be manhood and not manpower. We could not foresee a day in which everybody, by virtue of technology, would have free time and the question would be what in the world he would do with himself. We believed that everybody could learn, a conviction since confirmed by the scientific work of Bruner and others. We believed he could learn all his life long; we considered that the efforts of the University of Chicago since Mr. Harper's day proved that. We could see that American education was enormously wasteful of time and money, that the lockstep did not accommodate individual differences, that a system based on time served and credits accumulated could only by accident provide an education, and that by wiping out this system, which we did, we could make it possible for people to proceed at their own pace, to drop in and drop out, and to continue to use their minds as long as they lived. But we thought there would not be many.

Except for radio, in which the University of Chicago had the oldest program on the air, and films, with which we began to experiment around 1940, we had available as a means of distribution only that which had originated with Gutenberg. The trouble with radio was that it was in the hands of the oligopoly that controls it today. The University of Chicago "Roundtable" suffered a fatal blow when NBC moved it to an impossible hour. The 7-Up Company had bought the half hour next to the "Roundtable's" traditional time and demanded that "Roundtable" be moved on the ground that it was not a "good adjacency." The trouble with films was that the so-called portable equipment used in the classroom had to be moved by a truck and operated by a graduate of MIT.

Thomas Jefferson thought that some were destined to rule the commonwealth; the others were destined for labor. We do not believe in this kind of natural selection any more. Samuel Johnson held that all intellectual improvement came from leisure and that all leisure came from one working for another. We know now that leisure can come from technology: machines can do for us what slaves did for the Athenians. De Tocqueville found that it was as impossible to have everybody educated as it was to have everybody rich. Now we do not think it idle to talk about the abolition of poverty. We are no longer bothered by these ancient prejudices. Our trouble now is that we are confused about the purpose and meaning of education and that we suffer from what may be called an Institutional Illusion.

A president of Harvard once said that he did not want to discuss what education was. As far as he was concerned he was prepared to call education anything that was going on in an institution that called itself educational. So a president of Sarah Lawrence said that every student should plan his own curriculum, which is the same as saying that education is anything that is going on in anybody that calls himself a student. What goes on in most institutions that call themselves educational is some education, some child care, some training, some vocational certification that calls itself training or education but is not, and, at the higher levels, some research. As for students, the Special Task Force that reported to the Department of Health, Education, and Welfare the other day said, "Most students entering higher education today are not academically oriented." If then they were to plan their own courses of study, such academic institutions as we possess would rapidly pass out of existence.

There is a fundamental, though not always sharp and clear, distinction between a learning society and a society in training. Learning, as I am using the word, aims at understanding, which is good in itself, and hence at nothing beyond itself. Training is instrumental; it may not require or lead to any understanding at all; it aims at the performance of prescribed tasks by prescribed methods.

This distinction does not depreciate specialized, technical training. Any society, certainly any industrial one, has to have it. A rapidly changing cybernated society will have a tremendous job of continual retraining on its hands. The only question about such training is how to give it effectively. There is no apparent reason why industries, occupations, and professions that want trained hands should not train them themselves. Including training in educational programs or institutions simply means that they work at cross-purposes.

Training, which is simple, direct, with an easily definable and defensible object, is easy and easily measurable. It may involve no higher mental faculty than memory. Learning, or education, on the other hand, is infinitely complicated, frequently unappealing, and not readily accessible to quantitative assessment. Hence the attraction of training to a man like the new United States Commissioner of Education, who proposes to chloroform whatever there is of general education in the schools and replace it with something real, vital, and interesting, namely vocational training. In an effort to make this more palatable he adds to the confusion by officially renaming vocational training: he calls it career education.

Training will always be seductive, if only because it puts little strain on the mind of the teacher or the student. The trouble is, as Dewey pointed out, it is always obsolescent. And the rate of obsolescence is higher now than at any time in history. René Dubos has remarked that the more technical a society is the less technical its education has to be.

Yet most programs in most institutions called educational are now largely technical. And the remarkable fact is that all pretense that the curriculum has any relation to technical skill or that the diploma or degree awarded on the completion of the program denotes possession of technical skill has been abandoned. We do not ask what a high school, college, or university graduate knows or what he can do. We merely inquire whether he has graduated. Educational credentials are helpful to harried personnel managers, who simply announce that persons not having the requisite credentials, though capable of doing the work, will not be employed.

As I have said, learning, or education, cannot be defended as a means to anything beyond itself. It has no predictable effect on the prosperity of states or individuals. We cannot say whether the United States is rich and powerful because of its educational system or in spite of it. As for the developing nations, we know that as countries develop, their educational systems and expenditures expand. We do not know whether this expansion is a cause or a result of economic development.

It cannot even be shown that literacy is always indispensable to economic development. The big biscuit factory in Hanover in West Germany, which is fully automated, is staffed largely by illiterate Spanish women who cannot speak a word of German.

We should ponder, too, the report made in 1948 to the American Association on Mental Deficiency by an eminent sociologist. She showed that the typical male moron earned as much as $3.50 a week more than the average industrial wage and that the female moron uniformly made more money than the normal woman industrial worker.

A cybernated world is likely to be one in which a few highly trained experts and a small labor force, whose qualifications are that they can see a red light or hear a whistle, can operate an industrial plant. We need education in science and technology in a scientific age not to train us for the work we have to do but to understand the world we are living in.

The report of the Task Force to which I have referred ends with an absurd question: "How can students be freed from the infatuation of American society with the form rather than the substance of learning?" The students cannot be freed of this infatuation until the form rather than the substance of learning ceases to satisfy those upon whom their educational, economic, and social future depends.

The real question is, why is American society infatuated with the form rather than the substance of learning? The answer must be that if you don't know what the substance is you have to be content with the form. Or if you are confused about the substance you can at least identify and seek the form. You may not be able to tell whether a person is educated, but you can always count his credits, grades, and diplomas and the number of years he has been in school. Since the war we have said two things: first, that education promotes the power and prosperity of states and individuals, which cannot be proved, and second, that the status of persons rises in proportion to the time they have spent in educational institutions and the number of diplomas they have, which may be true but which makes no sense.

We shall not have a learning society until we get over our infatuation with form rather than substance. I see no hope of this until the cost of confusion resulting from a preoccupation with form becomes so obvious and overwhelming as to bring us to the realization that form without substance is as wasteful as it is meaningless. Think of the prospects of a learning society if we were to do what I have proposed many times before, if we were to confer the bachelor's degree on every American citizen at birth.

This brings us to the Institutional Illusion. Institutions calling themselves educational are the only culturally accredited instruments of education. Their forms are the only ones that count. In the advanced countries they are largely custodial: they take up the time of the young until we are ready to have them go to work. Everywhere in the world the length of time one spends in educational institutions and the success one has in them are determined by one's socioeconomic status and family background. This means that the power and prosperity presumably promoted by an educational system are conferred upon those who already have the most. The educational system, in short, is a means of maintaining the status quo.

We see this most clearly in the case of the developing countries. Many of them spend a third of their budgets on schools and universities. They all find the bulk of this money going to perpetuate the advantages of that tiny fraction of the population which is at the top of the social and economic pyramid. The overwhelming majority of the children never get beyond the first few grades. They not only fail to receive any benefits from the expenditures on education, but also suffer grave indignities that might not be visited upon them if the educational system did not exist. The graded

curriculum degrades those who are unable to continue in it.
These are uniformly the children of the poor. It is not that
they are ineducable. The failure is that of the institution
and its bureaucracy and the rigidities inherent in them.

As Ivan Illich has said, "Educators appeal to the gam-
bling instinct of the entire population when they raise
money for schools. They advertise the jackpot without men-
tioning the odds." The odds against the poor in the educational systems of every country are such as to intimidate the
most hardened habitué of Las Vegas or Monte Carlo. The
dice are loaded. We must look forward to an immense de-
centralization, debureaucratization, and deinstitutionaliza-
tion if we are to have a learning society.

Here technology can help us. The electronic devices now
available can make every home a learning unit, for all the
family. All the members of the family might be continuously
engaged in learning. Teachers might function as visiting
nurses do today—and as physicians used to do. The new electronic devices do not eliminate the need for face-to-face instruction or for schools, but they enable us to shift attention
from the wrong question, which is how can we get everybody
in school and keep him there as long as possible, to the
right one, which is how can we give everybody a chance to
learn all his life? The new technology gives a flexibility that
will encourage us to abandon the old self-imposed limitations. They are that education is a matter for part of life,
part of the year, or part of the day, that it is open in all its
richness only to those who need it least, and that it must be
conducted formally, in buildings designed for the purpose,
by people who have spent their lives in schools, in accordance
with an incomprehensible program, the chief aim of which
is to separate the sheep from the goats.

The Open University in England, if it can hold off the
Tories and avoid suffocation from its credits and degrees,
gives us some intimation of what the educational future
could look like. The Open University is nothing less than a
national commitment to use all the intellectual and tech-

nological resources of the country in a coherent way to give every citizen, no matter what his background or academic qualifications, a chance to learn all his life.

In this country the University Without Walls, which is just getting started, under the sponsorship of nineteen colleges and universities, including Chicago, appears to be contemplating the same thing. The only trouble with it is that the tuition fee is $2,650, which is higher than the resident fee at the University of Chicago.

The other day L. E. Dennis, provost of the Massachusetts state college system, asking "What's at the other end of Sesame Street?" proposed a University of North America on the same lines.

Other technological possibilities are suggested by the agreement recently made between NASA, the space agency of the United States, and the government of India. It provides for educational broadcasting via satellite to some 5,000 remote Indian villages. Brazil has shown interest in similar arrangements. The United Nations has set up a Working Group on Direct Broadcasting to promote and follow such experiments.

Then there are cables, cassettes, computers, and video tape. It is reported that a cable system is now being built in San Jose that will have forty-eight channels. It is hard to accept the proposition that all of these must be dedicated to the kind of triviality that is now the common fare on commercial television. The San Jose people would have to make a tremendous effort to avoid using some of these channels— and we are told that many more are technically possible—for cultural, artistic, and educational purposes, and in particular for the discussion of political, economic, and social issues.

Of course I know there is little in the record of the American people to suggest that they will use the new devices I have mentioned for their enlightenment. I remember running into E. M. Herr, president of Westinghouse, forty-five years ago. He said he had been to a big meeting in Washington with Herbert Hoover, then Secretary of Commerce, which had been called to settle the future of radio. I said, "Did you settle anything?" Mr. Herr replied: "We certainly did. We decided there should never be any advertising on the air."

Therefore I do not say we will use the new instruments technology has given us in order to create a learning society. I say only that we can. We can have a learning society. Its object would be to raise every man and woman and every community to the highest cultural level attainable. The affluence of a world in which science creates wealth will make it impossible to plead poverty as an excuse for not trying to educate everybody. As for our pitiful record in the use of our free time, Arnold Toynbee, who has a long historical view, reassures us by saying that free time may be abused at first by people who have had no experience of it; but sooner or later we shall be able to salvage some of it for learning.

In such a society the role of educational institutions would be to provide for what is notably missing from them today, and that is the interaction of minds. Eventually these institutions would not be "processing" anybody for anything or awarding diplomas or degrees. The search for what have been called sheepskins to cover our intellectual nakedness, which has been necessary to gain status in an industrial society, has smothered learning.

In the coming age the university could be transformed into a contemporary version of the Platonic academy. It could be a center of independent thought and criticism, bringing the great intellectual disciplines together so that they might shed light on one another and on the major issues facing modern man.

So when Karl Jaspers proposed something new for Europe, a technical faculty in the university, he did not do so in order to turn out more engineers or to get ahead of Russia. He did it because he thought how to live with science and technology was the most urgent problem of humanity. It could be solved, if at all, only by forcing technology to wrestle with other disciplines and forcing them to face up to it. The place for such confrontation, if you will forgive the expression, is the university.

No doubt this would compel a change in the organization and personnel of the university, which is now a collection of specialists who appear to grow more narrow as they become more numerous. The statement of Victor Ferkiss of the Department of Government at Georgetown in *Science* a couple of weeks ago about what specialists in political science have done has the ring of truth. He said, "The great issues of politics have been left untouched not so much because of a quasi conspiracy in favor of the status quo as because of a trained incapacity to think in a creative, innovative, interdisciplinary way about social matters, an incapacity fostered by the entire process of professional socialization, now beginning even at the undergraduate level." If a trained incapacity to think is the result of university study, we should perhaps reexamine its structure and its purposes.

To attain full humanity is to reach the level of critical consciousness. This means understanding reality and understanding that men can and should transform it. The university is that institution which should lead in the achievement of critical consciousness. It must use and contain within it all the major modes of understanding and transforming reality. Thus the university would represent and constitute the circle of knowledge, in which everything is understood in the light of everything else.

Such a university could preside over the progress of the learning society.

A CALL FOR NEW MISSIONARIES [3]

SAMUEL R. SPENCER, JR. [4]

Samuel R. Spencer, Jr., president of Davidson College, delivered the commencement address on May 23, 1971, at Erskine College, Due West, South Carolina. The Commencement marked the end of the 132nd academic year at South Carolina's oldest four-year denominational college. The speaker was able to establish rapport with his listeners because he and many members of his family had come from "the red clay of the South Carolina Piedmont." Several of his relatives, including his father and grandfather, were graduates of the school. Too often addresses to graduating classes are filled with meaningless abstractions and advice packaged in clichés and generalizations. But this speaker chose to discuss matters of vital concern to the people he was addressing. His theme, "We must deal with conditions as they are, not as we might like them to be," had special meaning to the audience because Erskine was graduating its first black student. It is entirely possible that this theme was much more acceptable to the students than to some of their parents. Of course, Dr. Spencer was repeating a thought that many newly elected liberal southern governors have emphasized (see "Inauguration Address" by Jimmy Carter, REPRESENTATIVE AMERICAN SPEECHES: 1970-1971, pages 142-6).

Erskine is brier patch for me. More than a half century ago, my father also stood in or near this spot and received an Erskine diploma. My mother's father was an Erskine graduate of a generation before that. The red clay of the South Carolina Piedmont was my native landscape, and Winthrop graduates in South Carolina red brick schoolhouses nurtured me through the elementary and high school years. The majority of you are South Carolinians, and even those who were outlanders four years ago now have, as a result of your stay at Erskine, a stake in what happens to this state and region. Consequently, I speak to you of the Class of 1971 as South

---

[3] Address delivered at commencement, Erskine College, Due West, South Carolina, May 23, 1971.

[4] For biographical note, see Appendix.

Carolinian to South Carolinians, Southerner to Southerners, American to Americans.

To have the last shot at a class of graduating seniors is quite a privilege. I might be overly impressed with the responsibility of coming up with something weighty and significant if I did not know, from the experience of many such occasions, that the commencement address is hardly the most important part of such a ceremony either to the graduates or the guests. In true professorial fashion, I think I will turn this one back at you and begin, not with answers, but with a question. I grant that it is a somewhat prosaic question, not as imaginative as students might pose. My question to you is this: What do you think will be the most important continuing problem on which you will have to make decisions as a citizen during the next twenty years? Depending on your interests and points of view, you could legitimately name a number of things—ecology and the environment, war, space exploration, inflation and the economy, public health and welfare. But if the question were broadened to ask for a list of such questions, there is one which I believe almost all of you would include. At least I hope you would include it, for to me it will undoubtedly be the matter with which all of us will have to continue to wrestle—that of public education. Because of its significance, and because it bears on most of the other problems, I want to devote my parting shot today to education, especially as it relates to our own region.

This is not the first time the South has had an educational crisis. Public education as we know it today had just begun to get a foothold in the years before the Civil War. North Carolina had a genuine public system of 3,000 schools by the late fifties, but it was well ahead of the rest of the Southern states. Jefferson's ideal of free public schools in Virginia had never been realized. What public schools existed in South Carolina and Georgia were decentralized, and there was little progress toward a statewide plan. Louisiana, Florida, Tennessee, and Alabama had laws on the books by the fifties, but in 1859 the Alabama superintendent of education reported that almost half of the children were not going to school at all.

Most of these tender shoots were cut down by the cataclysmic events that began in 1861. During the years following the Civil War, education in the South was a shambles. The ravages of war and social upheaval left the region gasping. Hundreds of thousands of children, both white and black, had little or no opportunity for education. This was the era when a new invasion of the South took place, an invasion of Yankee schoolmarms who answered the call for educational missionaries to the former Confederate states. It was only when new state constitutions came into being during the Reconstruction period that the South established a system of universal public education, free to all persons of school age. It took another generation or more to build secondary schools, and the public high school did not reach some isolated areas until the 1930s.

Now a new educational crisis is upon us. An astute Supreme Court watcher could have predicted the probable shape of things to come in public education from court decisions of the 1930s and 1940s. But what shook most of the South to the roots was the 1954 Court decision. For seventeen years we have been wrestling with its consequences. It must be admitted that many of us have interpreted the Court's "deliberate speed" mandate with an emphasis on the adjective rather than the noun. The difficulties have been enormous, as hard-working members of local school boards in communities all over the South can testify, even when localities tried honestly and conscientiously to carry out judicial instructions. Now the Court has spoken again, and this time in a way which seems to intensify the problem. Again there is weeping, wailing, and gnashing of teeth; again fulminations are hurled against the Supreme Court.

Let's not waste our tears. It isn't worth a single wail or tooth-gnashing. There is no warrant for the self-pity in which we have too often indulged. It is true, of course, that the Supreme Court, in its latest decision, seems to apply sanctions to the South which do not necessarily bind others. But no matter. Of all regions we are the most fortunate. Strangely enough, the day may well come when Southerners, white and black alike, will rise up and call blessed the name of the Supreme Court of the United States.

Let me tell you why I think so. First, the Supreme Court did not create the problem. The problem of working out the destiny of a pluralistic society began when the first black men stepped from the slave ship *Jesus* onto the shores of Virginia in 1619, and therefore can be considered indigenous to our nation. The Civil War settled the question of slavery, but it did not settle that of minority citizens; nor did it guarantee to them the blessings of a free society such as education. For a hundred years the question has been thrusting itself ever more insistently upon us, and we would be agonizingly trying to find answers to it even if the Supreme Court did not exist.

Meanwhile the problem of the black minority, once considered "peculiar" to the South, has become a national rather than a regional one. Half of the black citizens of this country now live outside the South; one third of them are concentrated in fifteen cities. Our good fortune lies not in the fact that others are also having to take hold of such thorny questions as racial balance, busing, protests, proportional representation, and the like. Rather, it lies in the fact that the South will solve its educational problem, and be done with them while the rest of the country is still in the throes of the struggle.

Such a prediction about the future of southern education may seem to contain a rather large element of bravado. Let me cite three reasons why I consider it justified. In the first place, public attention is focused on education in the

South today as never before. For a region whose tradition of public education is relatively short, this is highly important. We have had a good demonstration of this in Charlotte during recent months. Sensing the obvious public concern, the school board began to televise a number of its meetings. Suddenly thousands of citizens who never had the slightest idea of what went on inside a school board meeting are regular participants. Furthermore, though the interest began with the integration question, it extends well beyond this to matters of curriculum, materials, and teaching methods. The educational program for junior high school students has become a major public issue, a possibility which would have been unheard of only a short time ago. The fact is that Southerners, faced with the necessity for reordering education in accordance with court decisions, have become interested in and concerned for public education as never before in our history. Long at the bottom of the heap in statistical measures of educational progress, southern states today are developing school systems which hold their own both quantitatively and qualitatively on a national basis.

It is also our good fortune at such a time to see the emergence of new and progressive southern leadership. For the most part, southern politicians have had a great deal in common with Lot's wife, preferring to look backward rather than forward. The men who have recently come to power in southern state government, such men as Reubin Askew of Florida, Dale Bumpers of Arkansas, Jimmy Carter of Georgia, Bob Scott of North Carolina, Winfield Dunn of Tennessee, Linwood Holton of Virginia, and John C. West of South Carolina, represent a new breed willing to assess the past with realism and the future with hope and confidence.

Our new governors are consciously writing "finis" to the old era. "The time for racial discrimination is over," said Governor Carter of Georgia. "No poor, rural, weak, or black person should ever have to bear the additional burden of being deprived of an education, a job, or simple justice." "No more must the slogan of states' rights sound a recalcitrant and defensive note for the people of the South . . . the era of defiance is behind us," added Governor Holton of Virginia. Governor West was speaking for the entire region, not just for the state, when he said in his inaugural address, "The time has arrived when South Carolina for all time must break loose and break free of the vicious cycle of ignorance, illiteracy and poverty which has retarded us throughout our history." This is not the moonlight and magnolia view of the southern past which has provided our traditional escape from reality.

The L .Q. C. Lamar Society founded in 1969 under the name of the man who tried to bring North and South together again after the Civil War is another example of new leadership within the South. Spreading rapidly through the southern states, the new organization is dedicated to the practical consideration of regional problems such as education, employment, housing, and health care. As one leader said at the Lamar Society conference in Atlanta earlier this month, "There is indeed a new voice in the South, a new spirit, greater hope than in a hundred years."

We are fortunate, too, in that we have already seen the worst in our educational crisis and are on the upgrade. I say this despite gloomy predictions in some quarters of increased tensions and even violence next September. No one doubts that there will continue to be incidents for some time to come. Many of the things that have happened have been shockingly unpleasant. Many have raised feelings on both sides of the color line to a high pitch. In the face of such developments, it is easy to become disheartened and to feel either that we are making no progress at all or that progress is so meager as to be not worth the cost.

Under such circumstances I think we have to take the long view rather than the short. It is obvious also that we must deal with conditions as they are, not as we might like them to be. Let me give an analogy from another field where we also have deep concerns, that of environmental pollution. Suddenly we are threatened by everything from foul air to poisonous swordfish steaks, and we must do something about it. But no one suggests that we turn back the clock to another era and abandon our technological and industrial complex; rather, we live with it and find solutions to the problems it has created.

This is the approach we must take to public education. Some of the difficulties look as formidable as the scaling of Everest. But southern cities which have had to take the lead, whether they wanted to or not, are demonstrating that solutions can be found—solutions that are not necessarily pleasing or convenient, but ones which allow education to continue and even to progress under the severe stress of social upheaval. During the past several years we have become accustomed to speeches and statistics out of Washington which discount the progress of social change among us. But those of us who live in this region know better. Harry Ashmore, a very perceptive southern editor, wrote recently that "the relative racial calm in the South today is in sharp contrast to the still recent past, and to the situation which prevails over much of the rest of the country. This is not, however, a return to the old quiet of stagnation; there have been profound changes in the region and, one way or another, there will be more." Willie Morris, erstwhile editor of *Harper's* and author of *North Towards Home,* agrees. A year ago Mrs. Medgar Evers, who left Mississippi after the tragic murder of her husband in the sixties, testified to the marked differences she found during a return visit there. As Benjamin Muse wrote not long ago, despite "the fashion among liberals to belittle the changes that fifteen years have wrought . . . we have traveled a long way since May 17, 1954."

Furthermore, despite the depth of our unlovely tradition of discrimination and prejudice, the change is coming

more easily for us than for others. We are still essentially
a rural area, with few large cities. Because vast numbers of
our children have been riding buses from rural homes to
consolidated schools for many years, even the emotional
issue of busing is less threatening to us than to the inhabitants of the asphalt jungles of the North and West. Slowly
and unevenly but surely nevertheless, we in the South are
bringing our school problems under control at a time
when the great metropolitan areas are mired in a quick-
sand of difficulties which seem to grow worse by the hour.
Perhaps the South can eventually help other areas find a
way out of the common morass.

Now a bit of corrective. I am neither naive nor un-
realistic. I do not claim for a moment that we are "home
free" or even near it. Putting blacks and white together in
a common school building by no means guarantees a spirit
of community among them. Experience thus far has been
more discouraging than otherwise. It may well take a generation, and certainly ten to fifteen years more, before the
relationship between the races in our schools settles down
to a more natural and unselfconscious one. There are other
problems too, and big ones. Teachers will have to be
better prepared and better paid. We must find ways of
lightening their burden; theirs is the most difficult and demanding job I know. There are curriculum battles to be
fought, facilities to be built, bond issues to be carried. Like
it or not, we will be occupied with the matter of public
education for a long time to come.

This is where you graduates of the class of 1971—you and
others like you who are graduating from hundreds of colleges which dot the southern landscape—come in. In five,
ten, fifteen years, you will be moving into positions of
leadership in your chosen communities as merchants, lawyers, bankers, teachers, preachers, or what-have-you. You
will be officers in women's clubs, candidates for the city
council, members of public commissions and boards. Al-

most without question and without exception, you will have some opportunity to influence the pace and direction of public education.

If you do not do something about it, you ought to send back the diploma you will receive today. Why? Because that diploma means that you have something special to give. In the first place, the fact that you have successfully finished college puts you in a privileged minority. Only half of the graduates of American high schools go on to college and only a quarter ever receive their bachelor's degrees. Furthermore, as graduates of a liberal arts college, you should have more than a modicum of important qualities that derive from the liberal education—a knowledge of man and his environment, a sense of history, and a discriminating judgment in the realm of values. Surely you, more than most, will have something to offer to the solution of educational problems in your communities.

But there is something else which you have to offer as well. You have been educated in the Christian tradition. Hopefully you are committed to a respect for the dignity of every human being. Hopefully your ideal is to serve others rather than yourself. Hopefully your approach to human problems is one of love rather than hostility. The events of recent years in southern communities clearly demonstrate that such qualities are as necessary to the solution of educational problems as professional expertise. The emotional antagonisms arising from educational questions have often obscured the real issues and thwarted progress—and I am not speaking just of antagonism between white and black. The hostility between white and white often matches or surpasses interracial tensions. If you can bring the calming influence of Christian love to bear on the heated disputes of our troubled times, you will perform a service indeed.

A hundred years ago when the South was an economic and educational wasteland, missionaries came from the North to serve her needs. Economically today, we are prosperous and burgeoning with industry and enterprise, but the need for wisdom, good will, and hard work in education is as great as it was in the 1870s. This time the missionaries don't have to come from the North. There are plenty of potential missionaries right here among us. If you have any doubt, I mean you—those of you who have been educated in the South and will now become an integral part of it. The chances are that you do not know where you will be, either literally or figuratively, ten or fifteen years from now. But when the call comes to you in some nameless town or city, as it surely will, to participate, to help, to give your time and your money and your effort on behalf of educating those who come after you, don't pretend that you are hard of hearing. Don't try to hide. You will be wanted and needed. If I may suggest a response, the best one I know is from Scripture: "Here am I, Lord, send me."

THE PUBLIC CHALLENGE AND THE
CAMPUS RESPONSE [5]

WILLIAM J. McGILL [6]

There are many signs of uncertainty, confusion, and even trepidation about the future of colleges and universities. Large, privately endowed universities such as Columbia, Princeton, Yale, and Boston are facing huge operating deficits. Federal grants are drying up. Investment yields are shrinking. Frightened by student unrest, many private donors have curtailed their giving. Faculty vacancies are not filled. Library budgets have been trimmed. Weaker departments have been phased out. The market is glutted with Ph.D.s. Teaching loads have been scrutinized and increased. Faculty tenure has been questioned, and on some campuses withheld for new appointees. Union organization and faculty collective bargaining are sought on many campuses.

Out of this climate grew a speech delivered by William J. McGill, president of Columbia University, at the thirteenth College and University Self-Study Institute at the University of California at Berkeley, July 15, 1971. Sponsored by the Center for Research and Development in Higher Education of the University of California and the Western Interstate Commission for Higher Education, the conference brought together college administrators, faculty, and students for a four-day consideration of timely and significant problems facing higher education.

Before the Association of the Bar of the City of New York on November 16, 1971, President McGill confessed, "I love to speak and I seek every opportunity to communicate with people who wonder what university life might be like in these troubled times." During the past eighteen months he addressed the American Institute of Banking, New York City (February 6, 1971); the American Personnel and Guidance Association, Atlantic City (April 5, 1971); the Commencement of Iona College, New Rochelle, New York (June 5, 1971); the College of Holy Cross, Worcester, Massachusetts (September 24, 1971); and the annual meeting of the As-

[5] Delivered at the annual College and University Self-Study Institute, University of California at Berkeley, July 15, 1971. In a slightly revised form, printed in *The Public Challenge and the Campus Response*, edited by Robert A. Altman and Carolyn M. Byerly. Quoted by permission.

[6] For biographical note, see Appendix.

sociation of Colleges and Universities of the State of New York
(September 30, 1971). His speech "A Requiem for Joe College"
appeared in REPRESENTATIVE AMERICAN SPEECHES: 1969-1970, pages
139-47. Lengthy excerpts of his speeches have appeared in the last
few months in *The Christian Science Monitor* and the *Wall Street
Journal.* Any of these speeches would be worthy of inclusion in
this volume.

The point of view expressed by the president of Columbia
University is unpopular with college professors who have vigorously
defended tenure as a bulwark of academic freedom. Nevertheless
what President McGill says should receive careful deliberation,
for he points to problems that every campus faces.

My responsibility this morning is to attempt to bridge
the gap between critics and defenders of the powerful role
which faculties have come to play in university governance.

I accepted this assignment for two reasons. First, when
I saw the panel of speakers, I realized that the rhetorical
level of this Institute might be fairly high. Thus some real
benefit might derive from talking sense about our problems
even if the effort demonstrated more good will than good
sense. Secondly, the 1970s will almost certainly prove to be
decisive in the history of American higher education. Nearly
all universities, public and private, are drifting into deep
trouble with their traditional support mechanisms. No one
knows how we can deal with the social, educational, and
fiscal problems that lie ahead of us. Accordingly, we must
try to remove such discussions from the highly politicized
context of public charge and countercharge, and seek instead to examine our problems with the realism and honesty so desperately needed and so seldom applied.

Our problem is the role which faculties play in university governance. I need not tell this audience how convo-
luted that role has become. The root of much of the difficulty is the great expansion of universities in the period
since the end of World War II. First there was the student
boom under the impetus of the GI bill during the decade
after World War II. Then followed the great blow to
American self-assurance delivered by the Soviet satellite

Sputnik as it circled the earth beeping out its message of technological superiority. The Federal Government immediately undertook an all-out expansion of American universities. New Ph.D. programs bloomed across the country as colleges and normal schools were upgraded. An extraordinary entrepreneurial growth began to take place in physical science, engineering, medicine, and social science. Federal grants made it possible for academic departments and individual researchers to build a research establishment of the highest order of excellence provided only that the university would give assurances that the required space was available. To make space available, the Government undertook major construction subsidies, and underwrote a large-scale physical expansion of universities. Everything grew at a pace that seems in retrospect to be almost incredible. Budgeted expenditures for institutions of higher learning were approximately $4 billion in 1955. This year they are estimated to be $27 billion; nearly a sevenfold increase in fifteen years. The volume of Federal funds channeled into colleges and universities increased from $500 million in 1955 to $4.4 billion in 1968. This is a ninefold increase in thirteen years. Our student census was 2.6 million in 1950, 3.6 million in 1960, and is near 7.5 million today. The recitation of these statistics becomes a dreary enterprise, but the sense of growth which they convey is overpowering, and of course it is fundamental to an understanding of the difficulties we face now and that lie immediately ahead.

The expansion of our system of higher education was not symmetrical and did not concentrate on the problems posed by a threefold multiplication of our student population in an interval of twenty years. The fact is that under the stimulus of Federal policies stressing quality of education and quality of scientific research, higher education became transformed from a system oriented toward undergraduates to one stressing graduate and professional accomplishment. Vast resources were poured into the growth of graduate departments and professional schools in the interval from 1950 to 1970. During this expansionist period Federal aid for instruction, research and student support increased regularly and rapidly year by year.

The intellectual requirements necessary to secure acceptance at this elite level of educational attainment also increased both in scope and difficulty. We developed an elite corps of star professors, famous for their outstanding creative work. A variety of blandishments and privileges was developed in order to keep these men happy at the universities of their choice. Thus the norm of expected treatment of faculty came to be set by the fifty or so top universities in the country. I observed earlier this year that during this expansionist period we found ourselves in cutthroat competition with other universities for a limited number of able professors, worried about our academic ratings, and wondering whether next year's growth would meet the standards set by our competition. We were literally frozen by the thought of becoming a second-rate university through the mere exercise of civilized caution.

Now in the three-year period since 1968 it has become evident that expansion is over. Projections of the proportion of the population reaching college age during the 1970s point to a 40-percent increase between 1970 and 1978 compared with an increase of 90 percent in the analogous period 1960-1968. Studies of production and employment prospects of Ph.D.s indicate an oversupply well into the 1980s. The economy is sluggish. Federal support is contracting. American universities have moved very quickly from expansion to austerity, from boom to bust.

Most of us are drifting into serious trouble. The growth of our student population is beginning to drop off, but the demands of society increase. At Columbia University, for example, it costs approximately $11,000 per year to educate a medical student. Our annual tuition next year will be $2,800 and many students will have to borrow to meet even that subsidized figure. Our costs are mandated by traditional patterns of education and research, as well as by the rapid growth of costly and sophisticated instrumentation. We have no alternative but to accept this pattern of increasing costs unless we wish to drop such work altogether.

Undergraduate students have become highly restive as we have sought to grapple with sustained growth and sudden contraction. Thus we find on all sides a rising cacaphony of criticism of the inadequacy of modern universities. Students, politicians, and even the general public denounce us as though we are all engaged in a vast conspiracy to oppress students and subvert the American way of life. Despite such criticisms and despite our evident inadequacies, it is perfectly clear that for more than two decades we have been able to fashion an academic establishment exhibiting the highest excellence. Excellence has been served to the point that American graduate and professional education is simply the best there is anywhere in the world. Now this sensitive and self-conscious educational establishment finds itself under attack. Funds and privileges are undergoing rapid constriction. Junior faculty see a void where once universities offered bright prospects for a career. We hear repeated criticisms of the tenure system, of the role which faculty are said to play in stimulating campus unrest, of the unwillingness or inability of faculties to discipline militant extremists among their membership.

All these headaches are rather predictable consequences of sustained expansion followed by sudden austerity. It is simply a fact that major educational reform will be necessary if we are to survive this decisive and austerity-ridden decade. Many faculty members have not yet got the message that faculty privileges must contract along with diminishing resources.

New Federal support is likely to come in the form of substantial cost-of-education grants brought by students. Such support will greatly increase the competition for students, develop new emphasis on undergraduate teaching and curriculum reform so as to attract students, and tip the power balance at universities in favor of student power as students seek to control the resources they bring to the campus. A new academic world is in the making, one that is likely to be particularly harsh for us all and especially so for our faculty colleagues. It is not surprising that we are beginning to hear talk of collective bargaining on campus. The union organizers are there, and their blandishments are perfectly obvious. "You don't need to tighten your belts just because the administration demands it. Organize! Together we can protect our salary rights and all our hard-won privileges."

Tenure is said to be pernicious because it removes the stimulus to work ordinarily provided by an uncertain future. Most legislators feel that campus unrest has been greatly amplified by professors, secure in their jobs, who felt themselves free to engage in antiwar political activities and to lead students in demonstrations or other expressions of dissent. My own experience is that the view just expressed, although widely held among political figures, is nevertheless wrong. Much of the faculty involvement in demonstrations against which I have struggled has come from junior faculty who are not secure in their jobs. These young faculty members paid a severe price for their moral principles. Preoccupation with student protest led them to neglect their professional duties and many failed to satisfy promotion committees when the tenure decision had to be made. Thus my experience suggests that tenure, while perhaps stimulating occasional political activism among senior faculty, has had a very obvious dampening effect on militancy among junior faculty. I am quite confident that young radicals at junior faculty levels will confirm this view.

The origin of tenure was based on two considerations. Teachers have always been paid poorly in relation to the rest of society. Moreover, they have been expected to follow

a standard of personal conduct much higher than we require of ordinary citizens. Tenure provided an incentive to
enter an occupation that did not pay well. It also insured
that school boards or trustees could not dismiss teachers
for what they thought or said. Tenure, in this sense, is
simply security of employment provided for a teacher.
There is a probationary period of two to five years; after
such preliminary scrutiny, he is granted security of employment.

The rapid organization of the teaching profession during the last decade has made this concept of tenure outmoded and somewhat impractical. Collective bargaining
itself provides security of employment to the extent that
resources exist. Low salaries are being eliminated by bargaining for wages. Thus the question of whether teachers
who are members of a union need tenure seems to be one
that answers itself. Security of employment and wages are
matters for the bargaining table. The rules of orderly conflict between labor and management will determine what
kind of contract can be written.

Tenure as practiced in the fifty or so top colleges and
universities in the country is quite different. Security of
employment is of course provided by tenure, but the process also implies the self-selection of the faculty on grounds
of academic excellence determined by the faculty. The essential point is that tenure committees are faculty committees. Thus the faculty controls its own membership. Trustees and administrators sign papers and move approval, but
the decisive choices are made by the faculty.

We should begin by acknowledging that the system has
produced a faculty manifesting remarkable qualities of
excellence, probably unmatched elsewhere in the world.
But it has its problems.

The most obvious difficulty is an inability to amend or
rectify mistakes in judgment. Often these are very costly.
Tenure is granted to a faculty member on the basis of an
innocent-looking dossier displaying excellent academic cre-

dentials. Then it is discovered that the new appointment possesses qualities unknown and unanticipated by those who passed upon him.

When I was chancellor of the University of California, San Diego, we appointed a full professor from a university in Europe on the basis of an exceptional set of credentials. Shortly before his arrival a clipping was put on my desk indicating that this man had been arrested for inciting to riot in disturbances at his university. The prosecutor observed that the man had just been hired by the University of California, and moved to dismiss the indictment on the argument that to proceed further would simply make him a martyr. Our appointment, however, had gone through and nothing could be done about it. Shortly after our new professor arrived on campus, he emerged as a leader of the student SDS. He organized one agony after another, leading students in building occupations and other forms of militant protest. Finally we had to arrest him and he went to jail. By that time all sympathy for him on campus was gone. He has done very little professional work, and faculty members acknowledged to me privately that they felt the appointment had been a terrible mistake.

Our errors in judgment are rarely so dramatic. More often we find that we have appointed a faculty member to a tenure post without the knowledge that his capacities are hopelessly diminished by some personal problem: alcoholism, homosexual advances to students, or, more typically, a desperate neurosis that has the capacity to tear a department apart.

All these examples do occur, as you know, but they are hardly manifest evils of the tenure system. They are abuses or lapses of the system. A department or a faculty is in many ways a family, living in intimate contact with one another. They have the capacity to protect one another, or to irritate one another unbearably. Thus an essential consequence of tenure based on self-selection of faculty is that the greatest care must be taken in evaluating not only academic talents but personal qualities that are likely to have an important effect on the life of the faculty. But when universities are undergoing rapid expansion, the number of tenured faculty also expands very rapidly. Accordingly, service on *ad hoc* or tenure committees becomes an odious responsibility. It interferes with the serious work of the committee members, who often feel that they have better things to do. Tenure committees are easily misled by blizzards of propaganda from busy department chairmen who find it necessary occasionally to stretch the truth just a bit in order to meet staffing requirements. No chairman wants to lose an FTE for his department through inaction.[7] During our expansionist period, senior faculty members were often hired sight unseen by departments. Often enough the result was appalling, but it was too late to rectify the mistake. Rarely was a faculty member brought out to the campus for a few days so that he might be looked over by the deans and the president or chancellor. There wasn't enough money and there wasn't enough time. Errors of judgment tend to multiply with the rapid growth of higher education. Men with large reputations on paper sometimes turn out to have paper reputations, but tenure now gives us no opportunity to correct such errors.

It seems clear to me that our selection system for faculty has been weak because it has been operating under high pressure and without opportunity to correct mistakes. My general position is that the concept of tenure is too valuable to destroy, but also that we can no longer tolerate a ritualistic inability to deal with our problems at a time when universities are in great stress and under considerable public attack. Faculty committees and departmental selection committees must be willing to take their responsibilities seriously.

One interesting possibility is a second level of tenure review between the ages of fifty to fifty-five. When it is apparent that a man has not been contributing effectively to a university and has become either emotionally incapacitated or in-

---

[7] FTE is the abbreviation for full time equivalent faculty. A department is assigned staff members on the basis of its FTE.

tellectually dead, he might then be slated for early retirement, perhaps at age fifty-five. This could create difficulties in financing retirement, but in view of experience outside the teaching profession, I do not believe that such problems are insuperable. In fact it seems clear that practical plans can be developed. The greatest advantage of the second tenure review is that it enables faculties to maintain their standards of excellence if indeed they have the will to do so. Of course it will increase the committee work and will force faculty to make hard judgments affecting the lives of old friends. On the other hand the alternative is the loss of the tenure system altogether. It would seem far more preferable to attempt to perfect it than to sit back stubbornly defending abuses that will inevitably lead to the destruction of the idea that the faculty are the university.

There are other weaknesses of the tenure system as presently practiced. Because of the nature of the tenure committee review and because of the time pressures surrounding it, very strong emphasis is put on research productivity. Academics are understandably impressed by qualities of mind revealed in written form. One of the saddest figures on campus is the man who has everything but cannot get it out because of a writing block. Nevertheless, the tendency to measure scholarly attainment by written output favors the appointment of people whose interests lie primarily with research rather than undergraduate teaching.

This problem is often handled very simplistically by our political friends. There is no dichotomy between research and teaching. There is no reason for supposing that a faculty member who writes and thinks cannot also teach. The point is that we have created a reward system stressing narrow involvement with a limited number of advanced graduate students in preference to the drudgery of writing textbooks and teaching undergraduate classes. This weakness is evident to all of us. It is a predictable consequence of a public policy that has stressed research excellence for more than fifteen years. Nevertheless, it is possible to measure teaching effectiveness by using student evaluations to point tenure committees to the best teachers. In view of our new-found concerns about the state of undergraduate education, measures of teaching ability ought to be made a necessary component of every academic dossier. More important, it is now essential that we create and fund a series of distinguished teaching professorships in order to stimulate the reform that we all seem to want. This is an area in which new Federal funding and a new Federal policy would be exceptionally helpful to universities.

Certainly one of the greatest limitations of the current tenure system is the acknowledged unwillingness of faculties to deal with their militant extremists. Most faculties are understandably prepared to accord the widest latitude of expression to their membership. Privately they complain to administrators about the political activities of certain of their colleagues who seem not to understand or care about the ethical constraints which most faculty accept as unwritten law. Publicly they are unwilling to act. This attitude has been conditioned by a number of landmark academic freedom cases that any faculty member can recite. In recent years such cases are found chiefly in public institutions where efforts are sometimes made to remove faculty members because of public objection to their political views, or because of the character of their thought.

I was a party to one of the most famous of these cases, involving the philosopher Herbert Marcuse. He is a self-professed Marxist and something of an aging hero to the youthful devotees of the New Left. They do not trust anyone over thirty except possibly Mao or, to a lesser extent, Marcuse. I found it odd that Marcuse characterized himself as a Marxist. True, he thinks in dialectical terms and looks for revolutionary change, but it always seemed to me that his writings were interesting because of his efforts to take the necessary steps beyond Freud's enslavement in nineteenth century social norms, and because very early, and long before it happened, he predicted the rejection phenomenon that would arise among students in a technological society.

Marcuse, as I saw him, was nearly always a model scholar. Occasionally before a crowd he would get carried away and announce himself as on strike when he had already applied for a leave of absence, but he was a professor in the classical German style, searching for truth in his own way. When it was discovered in 1968 that Marcuse was teaching on the San Diego campus of the University of California, much of Southern California rose in a unified effort to remove him. The American Legion offered to buy up his contract. There is no doubt that the state administration was embarrassed by his presence and sought actively to secure his removal.

In such circumstances it is absolutely necessary to provide a bulwark of principle against irrational public attack upon a man for what he believes or teaches. Interestingly enough, Marcuse did not have the protections of tenure, but managed nevertheless to be reappointed over the objections of much of San Diego County, much of the legislature, and much of the state administration.

This is not the issue at hand. The issue is faculty militancy. Can we justify under any reasonable interpretation of academic freedom a professor who leads a group of militant students in the forceable occupation of laboratory space, making it impossible for others to work and certainly infringing on their rights? Can we justify a professor who does this wearing a paper bag over his head with holes cut out for the eyes in order to prevent identification, and who publicly denies his participation while admitting privately to colleagues that he was indeed there?

What are we to think of a man whose standards of intellectual honesty permit him to commit such acts, and what are we to think of colleagues who protect him in a lie when truth is the focal ideal of their profession?

This incident actually happened, to my personal knowledge, not very long ago. On another occasion, a professor marched in the midst of a group of militant students who forceably barred me from access to my office, and then denied on the witness stand in court that he was involved. My friends on the faculty observed this sadly and commented to me privately that it was very troublesome to see the state to which our profession had sunk, but they would not speak out publicly against it.

A faculty member at UC—San Diego once attacked me during a tense confrontation in the free-speech area using the vilest obscenities. Another faculty member who heard about it circulated a note to the faculty asking whether they would permit such behavior from their own membership. Nothing was done.

I understand their reluctance to act. It involves an unwillingness to be engaged in ugliness; an unwillingness to grapple in the dirt. Most faculty are gentlemen who hate conflict. When this kind of thing happens they diminish their sense of personal guilt by telling the president or the chancellor privately how much they sympathize with him for what he must bear, but they cannot bring themselves to stop it.

I think it is now necessary and important for faculties to develop explicit codes of faculty responsibility and professional conduct, matching the codes of privilege and tenure developed long ago. The major professions in this country have always imposed such codes of professional conduct on their members in order to uphold the integrity of their professions. University faculties must do it, and the tenure system cannot be a barrier to the development of this new sense of responsibility. The alternative is that the tenure system and the academic life will eventually be destroyed by an unwilling alliance of militant extremists among the faculty and powerful antagonists in political life who find that attacks on universities provide a sure road to popularity with the voters.

One of the historic anomalies of American education is that teachers have always been expected to pursue their profession for rewards other than money and to follow a standard of personal conduct higher than that practiced by the community. As I have indicated, circumstances are now changing. Salaries are improving, and some, not many, but some professors engage in activities that violate not only any reasonable standard of professional conduct, but even the law. Even given these exceptions, however, the rule of low pay and high standards continues. Most automobile salesmen make more money than most professors, and most people still expect professors to be the benign and attractive figures decreed by the stereotypic ideal.

As you know, academics are not noble men. They work in circumstances in which few people, even in their own professions, understand or read anything they do. They have feuds and sometimes use class time to denounce their enemies before puzzled and bored students who haven't the faintest idea what the battle is about. Professors are imperfect. Most of them are isolated from the rigors of the marketplace and from face-to-face adversary conflict. They tend to depend too heavily on principle; they rarely give themselves up to reasonable compromise, and they overreact to small irritations. But they have been the center of my life for all my adult years and I know of no more stimulating, attractive or idealistic group anywhere in our society.

The issue is not whether they are supermen, but whether in virtue of the fact that they are professors in contact with immature minds and serving as models for our young people, we have a right to expect a standard of behavior from them much higher than that followed in the community at large. More particularly, the issue is whether society has the right, consistent with its view of personal conduct expected from professors, to restrict them in the freedom of their lives or the exercise of their political rights.

Clearly, the principle when stated explicitly is repressive and fundamentally objectionable. We want professors to behave. We are now demanding that the profession discipline itself, but we cannot legislate rules of conduct for professors that in any way restrict what they may believe, advocate, or teach. We have been through all this so many times and one would have thought that by now we had learned that correction of abuses of freedom via repressive legislation leads to evils far more objectionable than those cited in the original complaint.

Most people cannot understand why public funds should be used to pay the salary of a Marxist professor who happens to believe in his heart that American society is evil. Why do we actually pay someone who teaches that the social order which supports him must eventually be destroyed and replaced by an ideal state meeting his moral prescription? It is very difficult for any taxpayer, oppressed as he is, to dig down for the funds that support such nonsense. Nevertheless, any thoughtful and sophisticated electorate must consider the alternative. If we do not accord a professor the right to teach and practice what he believes, rights fully guaranteed by our Constitution, then who will be able to teach anything but the orthodoxy prescribed as acceptable by the dominant political forces? In that circumstance the American Legion would be well advised to buy up Marcuse's contract, and Marcuse would be equally well advised to sell the termination of his services to the highest bidder.

It is all so obvious. Academic freedom is not an absolute right conferred from heaven or guaranteed by the Constitution. It is a form of tolerance exercised by society at large in behalf of those whose profession it is to think and teach, and who happen, in the exercise of that profession, to disagree with the substance and the direction of the society that supports them. The nature of such tolerance and its continued exercise require that professors manifest their disagreements by adhering to the highest standards of integrity and intellectual honesty. If they do this, they must be protected from political opportunists who seek personal advantage from their removal. If, on the other hand, members of the academic profession fail to conduct themselves according to such high standards, they should and must be disciplined by the profession itself.

Society cannot bar them from the exercise of their rights as citizens. It cannot establish special standards for teachers not set forth for other citizens. The academic profession can and should demand that its members follow a standard of conduct stressing the central values of the academic life: personal integrity and intellectual honesty. These values derive from the fact that we represent ourselves as a community of seekers after truth.

No governor, no board of regents, no university president can impose this standard upon us. We must impose it on ourselves or one day soon we shall find that all our professional standards are determined by lawyers across the bargaining table.

APPENDIX

BIOGRAPHICAL NOTES

ABZUG, BELLA SAVITSKY (1920-   ). Born, New York City; B.A., Hunter College, 1942; LL.B., Columbia University, 1947; editor, *Columbia Law Review;* specialist in labor law; lawyer for American Civil Liberties Union actions and other civil liberties cases; peace movement organizer; founder of Coalition for a Democratic Alternative, which supported the presidential candidacy of Eugene McCarthy, 1968; elected to United States House of Representatives (Democrat, New York), 1970; defeated in primary, 1972; member, House Government Operations and Public Works Committee; organizer Political Caucus for Women, 1971-   . (See also *Current Biography: July 1971.*)

CHISHOLM, SHIRLEY (1924-   ). Born, Brooklyn, New York; B.A., Brooklyn College, 1946; M.A., Columbia University, 1952; Professional Diploma in Supervision and Administration, Columbia University, 1960; member, debating society, Brooklyn College; nursery school teacher and director, 1946-53; director, Hamilton-Madison Child Care Center, New York, 1953-59; educational consultant, Division of Day Care, Bureau of Child Welfare, New York City, 1959-64; member, New York State Legislature, 1965-68; United States House of Representatives (Democrat, New York), 1969-   . (See also *Current Biography: October 1969.*)

COLE, EDWARD N. (1909-   ). Born, Marne, Michigan; attended Grand Rapids Junior College; attended General Motors Institute, Flint, Michigan; assigned to special engineering project at Cadillac; chief design engineer, 1943; chief engineer, 1946; other positions, 1946-50; chief engineer, Chevrolet Motor Division, 1952-56; general manager, 1956-61; vice president, General Motors, 1956-61; elected, member of Board of Directors, 1961; executive vice president, 1965; president and chief operating officer, 1967; chairman, Executive Committee, January 1, 1972-   ; chairman, National Industrial Pollution Control Automotive Sub-

Council of United States Department of Commerce; member, United States Secretary of State's Advisory Committee for the 1972 United Nations Conference on the Human Environment; member, Board of Trustees of Mayo Foundation; active in Detroit community affairs.

EDWARDS, GEORGE (1914-   ). Born, Dallas, Texas; B.A., Southern Methodist University, 1933; M.A., Harvard University, 1934; J.D., Detroit College of Law, 1949; representative, UAW-CIO, 1937; director, welfare department, Detroit, 1938-39; director and secretary, Detroit Housing Commission, 1940-41; member, Detroit Common Council, 1941-49; president, 1945-49; admitted to Michigan bar, 1944; with private law firms, 1946-51; probate judge, Wayne County Juvenile Court, 1951-54; circuit judge, Third Judicial Circuit, Wayne County, 1954-56, justice, Supreme Court of Michigan, 1956-62; commissioner of police, Detroit, 1962-63; judge, United States Court of Appeals, Sixth Circuit, 1963-   ; award for outstanding achievement in juvenile rehabilitation from Veterans of Foreign Wars, 1953; other awards for juvenile work; Phi Beta Kappa; author, *The Police on the Urban Frontier,* 1968; articles on crime and delinquency.

ELSON, EDWARD LEE ROY (1906-   ). Born, Monongahela, Pennsylvania; B.A., Asbury College, 1928; M.Th., 1931; graduate study, 1932-33, and L.H.D., University of Southern California, 1954; ordained, Presbyterian minister, 1930; assistant minister and interim, First Church, Santa Monica, 1929-31; minister, First Presbyterian Church, La Jolla, San Diego, California, 1931-41; pastor, National Presbyterian Church, Washington, D. C., 1946-   ; chaplain, United States Senate, 1969-   ; member, Committee of John F. Kennedy Center for the Performing Arts; chaplain during World War II, receiving several decorations; Freedom Foundation Award, 1951, 1954, 1957, 1958, 1959, 1960, 1962, 1964; Clergy-Churchman of Year citation, 1954; author, *One Moment With God,* 1951; other religious books and articles. (See also *Current Biography: November 1967.*)

HARRIS, JAMES G. (1913-   ). Born, Little Rock, Arkansas; B.A., Louisiana Baptist College, 1935; Th.M. and M.R.E., Southwestern Baptist Theological Seminary, 1939; D.D., Ouachita Baptist University, 1956; ordained, Baptist minister, 1933; First Baptist Church, Bunkie, Louisiana, 1940-45; Calvary Baptist Church, Birmingham, Alabama, 1945-48; Beech Street Baptist Church, Texarkana, Arkansas, 1948-54; University Baptist Church, Fort Worth, Texas, 1954-   ; various denominational posts in Baptist church administration in Alabama, Arkansas, Louisiana, and Texas; NBC Radio Network, Christmas Service, 1963; "Columbia Church of the Air," CBS Radio Network, 1965; contributor to *Southwestern Journal of Theology*, 1967; *Zondervan's Minister's Manual;* other religious publications.

HUTCHINS, ROBERT MAYNARD (1899-   ). Born, Brooklyn, New York; A.B., Yale, 1921; honorary A.M., 1922; LL.B., magna cum laude, 1925; dean, Yale Law School, 1928-29; president, University of Chicago, 1929-44; chancellor, 1944-51; associate director, Ford Foundation, 1951-54; chairman and chief executive officer, Fund for the Republic and Center for the Study of Democratic Institutions, Santa Barbara, California, 1954-   ; in ambulance service, United States Army, 1917-19; Italian Army, 1918-19; decorated Croce di Guerra (Italian), 1918; member of numerous honorary and learned societies, including Phi Beta Kappa, Order of the Coif; author, *The Higher Learning in America,* 1936; numerous other books and magazine articles. (See also *Current Biography: February 1954.*)

JORDAN, VERNON E., JR. (1935-   ). Born, Atlanta, Georgia; B.A., DePauw University, 1957; first prize, Indiana Interstate Oratorical Contest, sophomore year; LL.D., Howard University, 1960; circuit vice president of American Law Students Association while at Howard University; helped to desegregate the University of Georgia; clerk in law office of civil rights attorney Donald Hollowell; field secretary, Georgia branch of NAACP, 1962; set up law partnership in Arkansas in 1964 with another civil rights lawyer, Wiley A. Barnton, 1964; director, Voter Education Project for the Southern Regional Council, 1964-68; executive director, United Negro College Fund, 1970-72; director, National Urban League, January 1972-   ; member, Arkansas and Georgia Bar associations; United States Supreme Court Bar; American Bar Association; member, Common Cause; Rockefeller Foundation; Twentieth Century Fund; other service organizations; has held fellowships

202 Representative American Speeches

at Harvard University's Institute of Politics, the John F. Kennedy School of Government, and the Metropolitan Applied Research Center. (See also *Current Biography: February 1972*.)

KEELER, WILLIAM WAYNE (1908-   ). Born, Dalhart, Texas; student, University of Kansas, 1926-29; served as assistant chemist for Phillips Petroleum Company, 1924; presently chairman of the Board of Directors; special consultant, United States Secretary of Interior, 1961; member, Commission on Rights, Liberties and Responsibilities of American Indian; principal chief, Cherokee Nation, 1949; elected, Oklahoma Hall of Fame, 1966; Distinguished Service Citation, University of Oklahoma, 1969; chosen by Civitan International as one of five outstanding citizens in North America; served on various government committees, including presently National Parks Centennial Commission and Business and Industry Committee of the President's Council on Physical Fitness and Sports; founder, Cherokee Foundation; elected principal chief of Cherokees, 1971.

KENNEDY, EDWARD M. (1932-   ). Born, Boston, Massachusetts; B.A., Harvard University, 1956; International Law School, The Hague, Holland, 1958; LL.B., University of Virginia, 1959; United States Senate (Democrat, Massachusetts) 1962-   ; member, Senate Committee on the Judiciary; Committee on Labor and Public Welfare; Special Committee on Aging; Select Committee on Nutrition and Human Needs; member, Board of Trustees, Children's Hospital Medical Center (Boston); Boston University; John F. Kennedy Library; Boston Symphony; Lahey Clinic; John F. Kennedy Center for the Performing Arts; Museum of Science (Boston); Robert F. Kennedy Memorial Foundation; president, Joseph P. Kennedy, Jr., Foundation; United States Army, 1951-53; named one of ten outstanding young men, United States Junior Chamber of Commerce, 1967; author, *Decisions for a Decade*, 1968; contributor to magazines and journals. (See also *Current Biography: September 1963*.)

McGILL, WILLIAM JAMES (1922-   ). Born, New York City; A.B., Fordham College, 1943; M.A., Fordham University, 1947; Ph.D., Harvard University, 1953; instructor, Fordham University, 1947-48; teaching fellow, Harvard University, 1949-50; instructor,

Boston College, 1950-51; staff member, Lincoln Laboratory (MIT), 1951-54; assistant professor, Massachusetts Institute of Technology, 1954-56; assistant professor, Columbia University, 1956-58; associate professor, 1958-60; professor, 1960-65; professor, University of California, San Diego, 1965-68; chancellor, 1968-70; president, Columbia University, 1970-   ; Phi Beta Kappa, Fordham College; elected to Society of Experimental Psychologists, 1962; Governing Board, the Psychonomic Society, 1965; Board of Trustees, Psychometric Society, 1967; fellow, American Psychological Association and American Association for the Advancement of Science; Achievement Award, Fordham University, 1968; author of more than thirty-five scholarly studies and reviews; associate editor, *Journal of the Mathematical Society; Perception and Psychophysics.* (See also *Current Biography: June 1971.*)

MINK, PATSY TAKEMOTO (1927-   ). Born, Maui, Hawaii; B.A., University of Hawaii, 1948; J.D., University of Chicago, 1951; admitted to Hawaii bar; private practice in Honolulu, 1953-65; professor of business law, University of Hawaii, 1952-56, 1959-62; attorney, territorial legislature, 1955; member, Territory of Hawaii House of Representatives (Democrat), 1956-58; Senate, 1958-59; State of Hawaii Senate, 1962-64; United States House of Representatives, 1965-   ; member, House Education and Labor Committee; Interior and Insular Affairs Committee; Oversight Subcommittee on Poverty; Oversight Subcommittee on Elementary-Secondary Education; named Outstanding Woman in Politics, 1965; Pacific Speech Association Community Speaker of the Year, 1968; Honolulu NAACP Freedom Fund and Recognition Award, 1971; St. Louis YWCA Distinguished Humanitarian Award, 1972; Rehabilitation Services Medallion, 1971. (See also *Current Biography: September 1968.*)

NADER, RALPH (1934-   ). Born, Winsted, Connecticut; A.B., magna cum laude, Princeton University, 1955; LL.B., Harvard, 1958; admitted to Connecticut bar, 1958; Massachusetts bar, 1959; United States Supreme Court, 1959; practice in Hartford, Connecticut, 1959-   ; lecturer, history and government, University of Hartford, 1961-63; lecturer, Princeton University, 1967-68; served with United States Army, 1959; Nieman fellowship, 1965-66; named one of ten outstanding young men of year by

United States Junior Chamber of Commerce, 1967; Phi Beta Kappa; author, *Unsafe at Any Speed,* 1965; and magazine articles. (See also *Current Biography: November 1968.*)

NIXON, RICHARD M. (1913-   ). Born, Yorba Linda, California; A.B., Whittier College, 1934; LL.B., Duke University, 1937; practiced law, Whittier, California, 1937-41; attorney, Office of Emergency Management, Washington, D.C., 1942; lieutenant commander, United States Navy, 1942-46; United States House of Representatives (Republican, California), 1947-51; United States Senate, 1951-53; Vice President of the United States, 1952-60; Republican candidate for President, 1960; resumed law practice, Los Angeles, 1961; New York, 1963-68; President of the United States, 1968- ; author, *Six Crises,* 1962. (See also *Current Biography: December 1969.*)

RUCKELSHAUS, WILLIAM D. (1932-   ). Born, Indianapolis, Indiana; A.B., cum laude, Princeton, 1957; LL.B., Harvard, 1960; admitted to Indiana bar, 1960; attorney, firm of Ruckelshaus, Bobbit and O'Connor, Indianapolis, 1960-68; deputy attorney general, Indiana, 1960-63; chief counsel, office of attorney general, Indiana, 1963-65; minority attorney, Indiana Senate, 1967-69; member and majority leader, Indiana House of Representatives (Republican), 1967-69; candidate for United States Senate, 1968; assistant attorney general, United States Department of Justice, 1969-   ; director, Environmental Protection Agency, 1970-   ; named Outstanding Republican Legislator, Indiana House of Representatives, by Working Press; Outstanding First Year Legislator in Indiana House of Representatives, by Indiana Broadcasters Association; Man of Year, by Indianapolis Junior Chamber of Commerce, 1967; author "Reapportionment—A Continuing Problem," 1963. (See also *Current Biography: July 1971.*)

SCHLESINGER, ARTHUR, JR. (1917-   ). Born, Columbus, Ohio; A.B., summa cum laude, Harvard University, 1938; member, Society of Fellows, 1939-42; Doctor of Letters, Muhlenberg College, 1950; associate professor, Harvard University, 1946-54; professor, 1954-61; member, Adlai Stevenson campaign staff, 1952, 1956; special assistant to President of the United States, 1961-64; Albert Schweitzer Chair in the Humanities, City University of

New York, 1967- ; member, Board of Trustees, American Film Institute; trustee, Twentieth Century Fund; recipient, Pulitzer prize for history, 1945; Guggenheim fellowship, 1946; American Academy of Arts and Letters grant, 1946; Pulitzer prize for biography, 1965; National Book Award, 1965; author, *The Age of Jackson,* 1945; *The Coming of the New Deal,* 1958; *Kennedy or Nixon,* 1960; *A Thousand Days: John F. Kennedy in the White House,* 1965; and other works. (See also *Current Biography: October 1946.*)

SPENCER, SAMUEL REID, JR. (1919-   ). Born, Rock Hill, South Carolina; A.B., summa cum laude, Davidson College, 1940; M.A. and Ph.D., Harvard University, 1946-51; United States Army, 1940-45; assistant to president, Davidson College, 1951-54; dean of students and associate professor of history, 1954-55; dean of students and professor of history, 1955-57; president, Mary Baldwin College, 1957-68; president, Davidson College, 1968-   ; Omicron Delta Kappa; Phi Beta Kappa; Fulbright lecturer, University of Munich, 1965-66; member, Commission on Liberal Learning, Association of American Colleges; Council of Presidents, Association of Governing Boards of Colleges and Universities; former member, Board of Christian Education, Presbyterian Church; former president, Southern Association of Colleges for Women; author, *Decisions for War, 1917,* 1953; *Booker T. Washington and the Negro's Place in American Life,* 1955; contributor to magazines and journals.

VON BRAUN, WERNHER (1912-   ). Born, Wirsitz, Germany; B.S., Institute of Technology, Berlin, 1932; Ph.D., University of Berlin, 1934; came to United States in 1945; naturalized, 1955; assistant to Professor Oberth, experimenting with small liquid-fuel rocket motors, Berlin-Ploetzensee, 1930; technical director, German Rocket Research Center, Peenemuende, Baltic Sea, 1937-45; with United States Department of Defense, Ordnance Department, as technical adviser at White Sands Provings Grounds and project director, Fort Bliss, Texas, 1945-50; chief, Guided Missile Development Division, Redstone Arsenal, Huntsville, Alabama, 1950-56; director, Development Operations Division, Army Ballistic Missile Agency, Huntsville, 1956-60; director, George C. Marshall Space Flight Center, National Aeronautics and Space Administration, 1960-72; corporate vice president for engineering and development, Fairchild Industries, 1972-   ; chairman, international sponsor committee, Robert Goddard Library Program, Clark University, 1965-   ; recipient, Distinguished Civilian Service award, Department of Defense, 1957; many honorary awards; author of numerous books on rocketry and space. (See also *Current Biography: January 1952.*)

CUMULATIVE AUTHOR INDEX

1970-1971—1971-1972

A cumulative author index to the volumes of REPRESENTATIVE AMERICAN SPEECHES for the years 1937-1938 through 1959-1960 appears in the 1959-1960 volume and for the years 1960-1961 through 1969-1970 in the 1969-1970 volume.

(5890)